Wait, I'm the Boss?!?

Wait, I'm the Boss?!?

The Essential Guide for New Managers to Succeed from Day One

Peter Economy,
Inc.'s Leadership Guy

CAREER
PRESS

This edition first published in 2020 by Career Press, an imprint of

Red Wheel/Weiser, LLC
With offices at:
65 Parker Street, Suite 7
Newburyport, MA 01950
www.careerpress.com
www.redwheelweiser.com

ISBN: 978-1-63265-164-8

Library of Congress Cataloging-in-Publication Data available upon
request.

Cover design by Kathryn Sky-Peck
Interior by Maureen Forys, Happenstance Type-O-Rama
Typeset in Crimson Pro, Drina, and Aquawax Pro

Printed in Canada
MAR

10 9 8 7 6 5 4 3 2 1

To my children:
Jack, Sky, and PJ

Acknowledgments

Many thanks to the Career Press team, including Michael Pye, Jane Hagaman, Maureen Forys, and Rebecca Rider. In addition, I could not have created this book without the stellar efforts of my literary agent Jill Marsal of Marsal Lyon Literary Agency—thanks so much for all your expert efforts on my behalf.

Thanks also to Kevin Daum for introducing me to the fine folks at Inc.com several years ago. It's been quite a ride!

And thanks to my personal editor and writing muse on this project, Sheila Wagner, for your support and stick-to-itiveness. I really appreciate it.

Finally, thanks to my wife, Jan, for putting up with my crazy, 24/7 writing schedule. This too shall pass. Aloha au iā 'oe. Maui nō ka 'oi!

Table of Contents

PART III: *Common New Boss Challenges*

Introduction

*Management is, above all, a practice where art,
science, and craft meet.*

—HENRY MINTZBERG, management professor

*C*ongratulations! You have been selected to be a manager
in your organization. As you begin your leadership journey, know that you have been chosen for good reasons. Your
boss has seen potential in you as a leader and believes you
have what it takes to move your organization forward.

And, make no mistake about it. Managers make a very real
difference in their organizations—they bring the weather.
According to research conducted by consulting firm DDI
(Development Dimensions International), organizations with
high-quality leaders are thirteen times more likely to outperform their competition. Not only that, but DDI's 2018 Global
Leadership Forecast reported that the top two challenges for
organizations today are (1) developing "Next Gen" leaders and
(2) attracting/retaining top talent.[1] It's therefore in the interest of your organization—of *every* organization—to identify,
train, and develop high-quality managers.

Managers like you.

But there's a problem. Most organizations do not train their
new managers.

According to an article in the *Harvard Business Review* by Jack
Zenger, CEO of leadership development consultancy Zenger/
Folkman, on average, managers first get leadership training at

age forty-two. This is about ten years after they began supervising people.[2] In other words, they receive no training in how to lead others for more than a decade after they were assigned the job of doing so.

According to Zenger, three specific problems arise when new managers aren't given the training they need to do their job—and to do it well:

1. **Practicing without training ingrains bad habits.** Although it would be great if every new manager automatically absorbed good habits from their manager, the simple truth is that lots of bad managers are out there. And these bad managers make poor role models. In fact, researchers have found that over 35 percent of professionals have quit their job because of a manager, and 15 percent of professionals are considering quitting their job because of their manager.

2. **Practice makes perfect only if done correctly.** The old saying "practice makes perfect" doesn't really mean much when you're practicing bad management. If you haven't been trained in how to be an effective manager, then you could very well be practicing the wrong approaches to management.

3. **Your young supervisors are practicing on the job whether you've trained them or not.** The simple truth is that when you're put into a management position, you'll try to be a manager—whether or not you've been trained to be an effective one. Again, chances are, bad management habits are being practiced and supervised employees aren't at all happy about it. This can have all sorts of negative effects on employees and the organization, from lowered morale, to decreased engagement, to increased absenteeism, and much more.

So, what can you do if you're a new manager who hasn't been offered any training in how to lead or be a manager?

Read this book. And then put what you've read into practice.

This book is a complete guide to all the things you need to know as a manager. And, although it's written with the new manager in mind, it can also serve as a useful refresher for *any* manager, no matter how experienced they may be.

Although technology and changing demographics have transformed the workplace in remarkable ways over the past several decades, the basics of managing others have largely remained the same. Employees know what they want from their managers, and they definitely know what they *don't* want. In 2018, LinkedIn Learning released the results of a survey of nearly 3,000 professionals who were asked this question: "What is the single most frustrating trait you have experienced in a manager?" These four specific traits of bad bosses rose to the top:

1. Having expectations that aren't clear or that frequently change (20 percent)

2. Micromanaging (12 percent)

3. Being aloof and not involved (11 percent)

4. Not fostering professional development (11 percent)[3]

In an article on LinkedIn explaining these survey results, leadership training expert Elizabeth McLeod weighed in on the #1 trait of bad bosses:

> A lack of clear expectations is the root cause of poor performance. Leaders often think they're clear, but the data tells us a different story. Employees need to know why this matters (the purpose) and what good looks like (performance expectations). Show me a leader who says, "I shouldn't have to tell them, it should be obvious," and we'll show you a team that isn't clear.[4]

This book is all about learning how to be a good boss—an effective, perhaps even great manager and leader. I hope you get as much out of this book as I put into it. For further insights into management and leadership, please take a look through my more than 1,500 articles on Inc.com (The Leadership Guy): *https://www.inc.com/author/peter-economy*.

I wish you well on your journey as a new manager!

PART I

SO, YOU'RE NOW THE BOSS

To add value to others,
one must first value others.

—JOHN MAXWELL,
leadership author and speaker

Becoming a new manager can be a nerve-racking and confusing experience for anyone who has never supervised or managed others. That, however, does not need to be the case. Anyone can become an effective manager given the right tools and some experience. In this Part, we will explore the basics of becoming an effective manager and creating a high-performing organization. Topics include

- What managers do
- Setting goals
- Measuring and communicating employee performance
- Creating a learning organization
- Building teams and teamwork

1

Managers Do This (Not That)

*Management is doing things right;
leadership is doing the right things.*

—PETER DRUCKER, management guru

There has long been a controversy of sorts about what managers do, and how that differs from what leaders do—if it differs at all. This controversy can be summarized in the preceding quote by management guru Peter Drucker. According to Drucker, the job of the manager is to do whatever assignments they take on *right,* that is, correctly and well. However, Drucker then suggests that the job of the leader is to be selective about the assignments that they decide to do—to do only the *right things.* (And, I assume, to do those right things *right.*)

Although I understand Drucker's sentiment, I personally do not believe that management and leadership are mutually exclusive. The best managers I know are also the best leaders. They combine both jobs seamlessly, transitioning from management to leadership—and back again—as required by the task at hand.

The word *management* has traditionally been defined as "getting work done through others." It's the nuts and bolts of running a team, department, or organization. *Leadership,* on the other hand, is considered to be something a bit more emotional—and inspirational. Consider these quotes about the power of leadership:

> *My job is not to be easy on people. My job is to take these great people we have and to push them and make them even better.*
>
> —STEVE JOBS, cofounder, Apple

> *You manage things; you lead people.*
>
> —ADMIRAL GRACE MURRAY HOPPER, computer scientist

> *The first responsibility of a leader is to define reality. The last is to say thank you. In between, the leader is a servant.*
>
> —MAX DE PREE, former CEO, Herman Miller

In this book, I'm going to give you the tools you need to become both a better manager *and* a better leader.

For many of you, becoming a manager might have come as a bit of a surprise. One day you might have been working on your own project at the office—a skilled individual contributor to your team—and next thing you know, *you've* been assigned to manage the team. All of a sudden, your job has changed completely. Instead of just doing the work, you also have to motivate and lead others to get the work done.

Chances are, you're going to be expected to learn how to manage on the job, without any formal management training. If that's the case, then you'll probably draw from your own experience—looking to your own boss for examples of and pointers on how to be a manager. You'll probably also take a look around at other managers to see how they manage and lead their people and their organizations.

You can also learn firsthand from skilled mentors or teachers about the right ways to manage people, how to get things done for your organization, and how to properly serve clients.

But just as you can learn from others the right ways to manage and lead, you can also learn the wrong ways to manage colleagues or teams. No organization is perfect, and examples of bad management can be found everywhere: from the supervisor who insists on micromanaging to the boss who fails to properly communicate with their employees.

Observe the managers you come into contact with, both within your own organization and in other organizations. Do they use intimidation and fear to get results? Are employees empowered and energetic when they come to work or do they seem disengaged? Pay attention to what you see and think about the different actions you would take in order to obtain the results you want.

If the manager does all the work an employee was originally assigned to do, or if a manager tries to make all decisions themselves, then that's not being helpful. Part of the job of any manager is to scale their impact throughout the organization. That's done by delegating responsibility and authority to employees and then holding them accountable for the work they've been assigned to do.

Before we get into the details of delegating work (which is covered in detail in Chapter 7), let's first take a look at the four things every great manager does.

FOUR THINGS EVERY GREAT MANAGER DOES TODAY

If you took a business class in high school or college, you may recall the four "classic" functions of management: plan, organize, lead, and control. The foundation of how a manager gets their job done is comprised of these four, and these basic functions can help you in your day-to-day management duties.

However, I believe that these four classic management functions fail to reflect the reality of the new workplace, which is based on an entirely new partnership between workers and managers. This partnership is much more collaborative than it was in the past, with employees and managers working together to achieve the organization's goals. The time when managers ruled the roost by bossing around their employees and instilling fear in the workplace is, thankfully, behind us.

Here are four things that every great manager does today.

Empowers

Remember the last time you were trying to do an assignment and your boss was questioning your every decision—constantly looking over your shoulder and asking you why you were doing what you were doing? This kind of micromanagement doesn't get the best out of employees. Instead, it causes them to shut down—they wait for their boss to give them direction for every move they make. Instead of being engaged in their work, employees simply check out. We'll take a much closer look at the sorry state of employee engagement today in Chapter 14.

Today's best managers empower their employees directly while establishing a corporate infrastructure (creating teams, skills training, and more) and culture that support empowerment. Whether or not your employees say they want to be empowered, it is vital that you create an environment that enables and encourages every employee to give the very best of themselves on the job.

Energizes

Managers know how to make good things happen—for themselves, the people who work for and with them, and for their organizations. They often bring strong technical skills, organizational ability, and work ethic along with them to their management positions. But the one quality that transforms good managers into great ones is this: they know how to energize others.

Have you ever worked for someone who added to your own natural energy? Perhaps they took you to a higher energy state and brought out your best performance by creating and communicating an inspiring and compelling vision of what your organization could be, and what your role was within it.

The very best managers inspire and excite employees and colleagues—unleashing the natural energy within them. They don't sap the energy from an organization like poor managers do, but rather, channel and amplify it. A twenty-first-century manager knows how to successfully transmit the excitement they feel about their company and its goals to employees, in ways that can be understood and appreciated.

Communicates

You may already know firsthand the kind of positive effects that are created for a business when managers know how to communicate effectively with their employees. In contrast, you may also be familiar with the negative effects that can occur when a manager fails to communicate effectively and well. When managers fail to communicate effectively— whether it's such things as making assignments, tracking project details, or setting expectations—they are missing out on a critically important role of management and are potentially reducing employee engagement.

Communication, the lifeblood of any organization, is a key function of the modern manager. With the speed of business today constantly accelerating, managers must communicate information to employees faster than ever. In fact, with today's technological advancements, managers have a wide variety of ways to communicate with their employees and get their messages across—email, text messages, tweets, video conferences, and more.

Supports

Your role as a manager is not to hover over the shoulders of your employees. Instead, it's to support them. Rather than being a strict watchdog or police officer, a manager must become a coach and cheerleader for their employees—inspiring them to achieve more and better than they ever imagined possible.

Supportive managers know that it's not all about shining a spotlight on their own achievements. They aren't hungry for everyone's attention. Instead, they shine a spotlight on the achievements of their people—providing them with the training and resources they need, as well as the authority they need to make their own decisions and get things done.

Sure, their people may make mistakes from time to time, but after all, how does anyone learn without making mistakes? What is critical is this: even if the employee falls down, today's managers reach out a helping hand and pull them back up.

WHICH MANAGEMENT STYLE SHOULD YOU ADOPT?

More than most positions, the way you choose to do your job as a manager can and often does have a tremendous effect on the people around you. One style of managing, for example, might get your people inspired, excited, and engaged in their work, whereas another style might cause them to tune out and shut down.

As a result, it's particularly important to choose your style of management wisely.

Think about how your current or former managers or bosses managed. What style did *they* employ on the job? How did their chosen approach make *you* feel? Your coworkers? Did it bring out the best in you and those with whom you worked, or did it cause you to shut down?

Let's take a look at three different styles of managing.

The Theory X Management Style

Do you believe management is something you do *to* people, instead of something you do *with* them? If so, you may identify with what is commonly called *Theory X management*. This approach to managing assumes that people aren't particularly motivated on their own to do their work. As a result, managers who are believers in this style may utilize intimidation and fear as a means of getting a response and results.

Be careful, however. Although delivering threats and ultimatums may bring about short-term compliance, it almost always results in a long-term decline in performance. Long-suffering employees simply quit and look for new jobs, or perhaps even worse, they chronically underperform—retiring in place.

Managers must take command of their organizations—that's an important part of the job—but in a way that doesn't shut down employees or disengage them from their work. So, make sure that people are accountable for results and that goals are being attained. But remember to maintain respect for and clear communication with your staff. After all, the majority of employees who leave their positions do so because of the negative actions of their direct supervisor or manager.

The Theory Y Management Style

Some people believe that *Theory Y management* is the best approach for managers to adopt. This approach assumes that people basically want to do a good job and can and should always be trusted to do the work. The manager who adheres to this style is sensitive to an employee's feelings, sense of self-worth, and tranquility.

As a manager, you may get a response with this approach, but you are not likely to consistently get the best possible results. Why not? Because there will always be someone (maybe more than one person) who takes advantage of bosses who adopt the Theory Y management style. They may consistently arrive late for work, call in sick, fail to meet their goals, and generally slack off. If the behavior of these employees is not corrected, then you're setting your organization up to fail.

Balancing Theory X and Theory Y

When deciding which management style to adopt, keep in mind that balance is key. The style of management you adopt can be situational, that is, it can (and should) change depending on the situation or the person you are dealing with. Being a balanced manager means removing company obstacles, creating a working environment that allows employees to reach their goals, and spending more time and energy dedicated to one of your most important jobs: inspiring everyone to do their best.

But it also means tracking employees' progress toward achieving goals, regularly meeting with them to determine why they aren't achieving their goals, and then helping them correct their performance. Employees must be accountable for their performance—or lack of it—and you as manager must hold them to the commitments they have made to you, your organization, your customers, and other stakeholders.

Ultimately you want everyone in your organization to feel like they are winning. Once you step back to let your employees do their jobs, you can deal with your business's organizational problems (e.g., bureaucratic obstacles, outdated systems, bad policies, and more). Although some employees may feel compelled to compete with coworkers for a piece of the pie, your job is to simply create a bigger pie for all to enjoy.

THE KEYS TO BEING A BETTER MANAGER

If you're selected to become a new manager, you likely hold some sort of expertise in the areas you are asked to manage. For example, you might be a bank teller who is selected to supervise other bank tellers. Or you might be a software coder who is assigned the job of leading a project team.

Once a doer, you are now responsible for being a good manager of doers. As you can imagine, this actually requires an entirely different set of skills than when you had to do the task on your own. You'll need to, for example, apply the skills of organization, planning, and leadership. To better understand what your new role entails, here are the keys to being a better manager.

Keeping an Open Mind

Companies that employ the old way of doing business—one that is hierarchical and does not encourage employees to bring their ideas and suggestions forward for consideration—do not stand a chance against organizations that value innovation and openness to ideas. You never know where the best ideas will come from, and it's often those people closest to customers who come up with the best ideas to address their needs. Encourage your people to experiment, take risks, change things up, and seek out better ways to serve others. Be open to new procedures and possibilities. When you do that, your employees will bring their best efforts to the table, and your organization and your customers will benefit as a result.

Taking the Time You Need to Make Good Decisions

Every business requires decisions to be made on a near-constant basis. Some decisions—say, whether an individual employee should start their break in ten minutes versus fifteen minutes—may have little impact on the business as a whole. Other decisions—whether or not to embark on a multibillion-dollar acquisition of a key competitor, for example—will have a large and long-term impact on the business and its employees, customers, vendors, shareholders, communities, and other stakeholders. Good decision-making is an essential business skill that most people unfortunately acquire only through trial and error instead of through practical training.

Your job as a manager is to make decisions. Some of the worst decisions are made when they are done in too much of a rush. Effective managers take their time when making a decision. They do not resort to overly quick fixes and they make sure to always consider their options. Management solutions can tend to be common sense, but what is challenging and time-consuming is transforming common sense into common practice.

Creating an Empowering Culture

The line between managers and employees was once clearly drawn, often through the use of fear and intimidation. But the landscape of the new business environment involves changes on a major, if not global, scale. As a result, employees at every level—not just the very top—are now taking on responsibilities that were once considered to be the sole province of supervisors and managers. When you create an empowering culture in your organization, you'll unleash the energy and engagement of each one of your employees, while encouraging your people to consistently give their very best efforts.

Building and Maintaining Trust

Trust is a two-way street. As a manager, you need to trust your people to do a good job. And, your employees need to know that they can trust you to look out for their best interests. When you build bridges of trust with your people, they will engage in their work, be willing to take risks, offer suggestions, and move your organization forward. If you want your organization to survive and thrive in the future (and I'm sure you do), then trust is the strong foundation on which to build it. Just be sure to keep tabs on employee performance and progress toward completion of goals. Trust, but verify.

2

Time to Set Some Goals

Done is better than perfect.

—SHERYL SANDBERG, COO, Facebook

The world is yours! You can go anywhere. In fact, if you do absolutely nothing, you will still go somewhere.

That wide-open world of possibilities may sound appealing at first. But as a manager, you don't want to go just *anywhere*. You want to get to a place of importance and meaning with your leadership—you want to go *somewhere*. To make this happen, the first thing you need to do as a manager is decide where it is that you want your organization to go. The next thing you need to do is formulate plans for getting there.

Let's say you envision creating a new product that you hope will gain considerable market share within a year after it is introduced. What kind of plan will help you attain the results you want? A half-baked approach with little to no planning? A prayer? Or a structured, goal-oriented plan? (I would put my money on the last choice.)

Still not sure what the correct answer is? Perhaps you need a reminder about the importance of goals. Here are the main reasons why you need to set goals in order to get anywhere significant.

Goals make your vision real. Whatever your vision is, you will have to get to it in multiple small steps. Don't expect to announce your grand vision on a Monday and have it achieved within twenty-four hours. If you want to achieve your vision, you must set and accomplish a series of small goals first before you see big results.

Goals lead to a purpose. Give your employees something to work toward. *Stretch goals* (goals beyond normal levels of employee performance) will motivate your workers, challenge them, and compel them to rise to the occasion when extra effort is required to achieve their goals.

Goals help you measure progress. How can you know where you are if you don't know where you have been—and where you are going? Goals are like points of interest on a map. As you make your journey toward your final destination, goals tell you how far you need to go and how far you have already traveled.

Goals help your people know what they are supposed to do. Discuss goals with your team so everyone understands how to use their strengths to help get there. Clarifying tasks, deciding who handles which tasks, and determining expectations for employees are all necessary steps you must take as a manager. They can all be achieved simply by setting goals with your people.

Goals give your organization direction. When you set a target to aim for, you are helping guide your organization to where you want to go. And as you translate your vision into goals, you are making sure you do not waste countless hours headed down a path you do not want to travel.

In order for goals to be effective, they must link directly to you and what you decide your team's final destination should be. To stay ahead of the competition, organizations create compelling visions driven by goals that employees and management work together to set and accomplish.

Remember, the best goals all share the same characteristics:

- They are attainable, but still challenge all involved.
- They are clear in purpose, definite and detailed, and are specifically few in number.

- They involve others. No goal at an organization can be achieved by one person! Involve others in your team to commit to and collaborate on setting and achieving goals. Doing this will set your organization on the fast track toward success.

SMART GOALS VS. CLEAR GOALS

The SMART goals acronym has been used by businesspeople for decades to describe the characteristics of the best goals, whether they're going to be accomplished at work or in their personal lives. Essentially, the SMART acronym gives us an easy way to remember and implement the most important elements needed in order for a goal to be effective.

Here's what SMART stands for:

Specific: Goals must not be ambiguous, and should be clear.

Measurable: You should be able to measure results in some way, for example, the number of new customers each month, or the percent completion of a specific task.

Attainable: Goals must be practical and realistic and able to be attained by the average employee.

Relevant: Your organization's overall vision must relate to your goals.

Time-bound: Goals have a fixed duration and have a definite beginning and end point.

We know SMART goals are supposed to lead you in the direction of all that you are hoping to achieve by asking that you be absolutely clear on what you are trying to accomplish.

However, SMART goals have simply not kept up with the times. An increasing number of businesspeople are coming to this realization, and so are, surprisingly, Olympic gold medalists.

Adam Kreek, a motivational speaker and member of the gold-medal-winning Canadian rowing team at the 2008 Beijing Olympic Games, knows a lot about setting goals. Now an entrepreneur, Adam believes that as most businesses now find themselves in a more agile and faster environment, the workplace of today requires a new method of goal setting. To provide a framework for action, Adam developed the idea of CLEAR goals:

Collaborative: Goals should encourage employees to work collaboratively and in teams.

Limited: Goals should be limited in both scope and duration.

Emotional: Goals should make an emotional connection to employees, tapping into their energy and passion.

Appreciable: Large goals should be broken down into smaller goals so they can be accomplished more quickly and easily for long-term gain.

Refinable: Set goals with a headstrong and steadfast objective, but as new situations or information arise, give yourself permission to refine and modify your goals.[1]

If you want to see successful results of your goal setting, you must be sure to adapt to the changing waters of the new, fast-paced markets we are seeing in the business world today. Consider using Adam Kreek's CLEAR approach to setting goals in the future. I'm certain you'll experience positive results when you do.

THE BEST GOALS ARE SHORT AND SWEET

Does the following situation paint a familiar picture for you?

Imagine you and your management team have scheduled several full days dedicated solely to strategizing for the long term.

You block out hours and hours to meet, throwing yourselves headfirst and wholeheartedly into developing a foolproof plan. Everyone talks about improving project turnaround and increasing the quality of customer service. Every member of the team tries to answer the same questions: *What are the organization's goals? How will the organization know when the goals are achieved?*

When the last planning meeting is completed, you and your managers circulate a round of "Congratulations!" while patting one another on the back for a job well done. Despite all this hard work, however, before long, the meeting is forgotten and business goes on as usual.

Don't let your efforts be in vain. When spending time and energy setting goals, be sure to keep them to a realistic number. There's just no way you can focus on more than a few goals—it's simply not possible. If the number of goals you have is manageable and you focus on a few at a time, you will be able to get them done before you move on to the next ones.

When it comes to setting goals, less is more.

But how do you know you are selecting the right goals for your organization? What about the right *number* of goals? These guidelines will help provide you with the answers to these questions:

Focus on two or three goals. Although we live in a multitasking world, it is still not possible to do everything all at once, and it would be foolish to expect your employees to do so. Only attempt to complete a few goals at one time, because setting too many goals will diffuse the efforts of you and your staff—leading to subpar results.

Pick relevant goals. There is only so much time in the workday, so focus your efforts on the goals that will have the biggest payoff for your business. Select goals that will bring you closer to what you envision for company success.

Focus on your organization's mission. Some goals are interesting, fun, challenging, and hard to resist. But if these same goals are totally irrelevant to your organization's mission, don't spend any time on them. Focus your efforts—and the efforts of your team—solely on goals that contribute to achieving your mission.

Revisit your goals and update them as needed. Business is unpredictable and full of changes, so regularly assessing your goals is an absolute necessity. Schedule quarterly or midyear reviews. If need be, revise company goals, because you will need to make sure these goals are still relevant and important to how your organization functions—not just today, but well into the future.

Goal setting and thinking about the future can be exciting. But when we get too excited about goals, we may create too many, overwhelming our people and ourselves. Remember that success in management involves meeting daily opportunities and challenges, not by measuring one success after another. Improve your organization by concentrating your efforts on a few significant goals, rather than many.

TRANSMITTING GOALS TO YOUR PEOPLE

How effective can a goal really be if no one knows about it? If you want a goal to be accomplished in a fast and successful manner, you need to let others know what that goal is so they can help you achieve it.

This is true in the workplace too. As you communicate your goals to your employees, make sure they are communicated clearly, are understood, and that everyone actually follows through on accomplishing them.

In addition to communicating your organization's goals, it is imperative that you also communicate your organization's *vision*—a picture of the distant horizon that everyone in the organization is working toward. You can communicate this as frequently as possible, throughout your organization, and to a wide audience of people (e.g., suppliers, clients, employees, etc.).

But there are some ways organizations drop the ball. Sometimes managers spend so much time developing a company vision that they become tired of it, rendering it boring and lifeless. Other times organizations are slow to communicate the vision, making it obsolete by the time it finally trickles down to front-line employees.

Show that you care about the vision by communicating goals with a sense of urgency and energy. Here are some ways

companies commonly communicate a vision to employees—
and to the public:

- Proudly asserting vision statements on corporate
  websites or other social media

- Branding their vision on tangible items like name
  tags, business cards, posters, and more

- Holding all-hands meetings for employees and unveil-
  ing the vision in motivational presentations

- Having managers bring up the vision in meetings or
  during recruitment conversations

In comparison to visions, goals are actually more tailored
to specific employees and departments. Use more direct and
formal means of communicating them. Here are some tips:

- Capture goals in writing.

- Introduce and assign goals in one-on-one or face-to-
  face meetings with your employees.

- Bring the team together in one space to introduce
  goals, explaining the team's role as well as the role of
  each individual. Make sure all parties involved know
  their responsibilities for the goal's completion.

- Acquire employee commitment to working toward
  the goals and ask that they prepare and present plans
  and scheduled timelines. Be sure to check in on progress and assist with any problems.

3

Want to Be Sure
Employees Perform?
Measure and Communicate

*In most cases being a good boss
means hiring talented people and
then getting out of their way.*

—TINA FEY, actress

Ultimately, your job as a manager—whether new or veteran—is to get things done through others. You do this by hiring great people, setting goals with them, and then getting out of their way. If they accomplish their goals, then they've proven they have what it takes to get the job done. You can then assign them more tasks and give them increased responsibility and authority, knowing that they'll follow through and succeed. If for some reason they don't accomplish their goals, however, then you've got a problem.

The question is, why didn't they accomplish their goals? Is some organizational obstacle in the way? Is the budget insufficient? Do your people lack the training they need to do the assignment well? Are employees in a different department creating roadblocks that you'll need to clear out of the way?

You'll hear the word *execution* often in the business world today. In business, execution refers to successfully following through with and completing a task. Essentially, execution is about transforming goals into action.

But how do you, as a manager, check an employee's progress in executing goals? What should be your first step?

First, you need to figure out what success looks like. How can you quantify a goal in ways that are precise and measurable? Measuring performance in terms of quantity is important. This eliminates employee confusion about the quality of their performance or if they need to improve. When you quantify goals, you make sure you don't leave anything to the imagination. Instead, you make it clear to supervisors and employees what goal execution looks like.

The nature of a goal determines how you monitor and measure an employee's completion of it. Goals can be measured in terms of units produced or delivery of product (for example, a sales proposal or a report) or in terms of time. For example, suppose your goal is to begin publishing a monthly company newsletter before the end of the third quarter. You measure the completion of this goal using the specific date the newsletter is successfully implemented. If your year runs from January to December and the newsletter is published in September, then the goal has been successfully accomplished. If publication of the newsletter is delayed until December, then the goal has not been successfully accomplished since the newsletter was published in the fourth quarter, not the third.

Recognizing an employee's incremental progress toward a goal is just as important as knowing when the employee reaches the goal. For instance, let's say the goal is for your floor salesmen to increase the average number of items sold from sixty to one hundred each day. Track sales progress and publicly post weekly summaries of each employee's daily transaction counts. Then praise employees' progress as they approach the final goal.

Here's the secret to measuring and monitoring employee progress and performance: give positive feedback. Giving positive feedback encourages your employees to continue with the behavior you want; giving negative feedback only discourages behavior you do not want. Here are some examples:

- Rather than measuring the number of backlogged shipments, measure the number of completed shipments.

- Rather than measuring the number of employee sick days, measure the number of employee well days.

- Rather than measuring the amount of faulty parts, measure the amount of properly assembled parts.

When it comes to whether you should make performance feedback for your employees public or private, put group feedback out in the open for all to see. You are more likely to get your desired results if you keep individual performance measures private and group performance measures (average days late, total revenues, and so forth) public. After all, your goal is to get your team to work together to improve.

Be careful, however, to avoid embarrassing individual employees when they have improvements to make. Instead, coach and counsel them privately to inspire better performance. They will appreciate it.

CRAFTING MEASURES OF PERFORMANCE

If you can't effectively measure and monitor goals, how will you or your employees ever achieve them? (Hint: They can't.) When you're designing a system for measuring employee performance against goals, there are four key things to keep an eye on: milestones, actions, relationships, and schedules.

Milestones

No goal should be without a starting point, a point of ending, or points in between that allow for progress to be measured. Checkpoints, markers, and events can act as *milestones* that tell you and your employees how much progress you have made and how much further you must go to reach your set goals.

For example, suppose you establish a goal of holding a corporate event in three months. The fourth milestone on the way to your ultimate goal of event completion is to submit a security deposit for a venue no later than March 5th. If the deposit is submitted on February 28th, you quickly and assuredly know event planning is ahead of schedule.

Actions

Actions are known as the specific activities an employee performs to move from one milestone to the next. Each action gets employees closer and closer to reaching milestones on the way to goal completion. In the previous example of a corporate event, reaching the fourth milestone might require the following actions:

- Researching available venues in the selected area
- Creating a spreadsheet comparing venue characteristics and costs
- Submitting the event budget to a manager

Relationships

Milestones and actions interact with each other through *relationships,* which shape the proper sequencing and order of activities you need performed on the way to goal accomplishment. Although a sequence is not always required, completing certain actions before others can lead to more effective and faster accomplishment of goals.

In the previous list of actions needed to reach the fourth project milestone, you want employees to submit an event budget with costs only after available venues have been researched and compared. These actions will then lead to selection of venue and submission of the venue security deposit.

Schedules

Be sure to determine how far apart milestones must be and how long it should take to complete a given project. Estimate the *schedule* of each action in order to plan better and establish a proper timeframe for project completion. How long should it take to put together reasonably accurate expenditure reports? Is the scheduling process for necessary meetings a lengthy one? Questions like these are important to answer when you consider how to meet milestones on time.

WHY COMMUNICATE PERFORMANCE TO EMPLOYEES?

Conducting regular formal performance evaluations for employees may sound like a boring or not-so-fun part of the job of being a manager, but it is absolutely essential. We all need feedback to know if we are performing well and to identify areas in which we need to improve.

Consider these opportunities that naturally emerge from the performance evaluation process:

An opportunity to talk performance past and future: Employees want to know if they are doing a good job. With formal performance evaluations, managers are encouraged (some might say forced) to communicate both performance expectations and results—good and bad.

An opportunity for career development and goal planning: Discussions about career development can take place in a separate forum, but the performance evaluation is a great time to discuss employee strengths (and weaknesses), and how the employee can use these to propel future career milestones and goals.

An opportunity for formal documentation: Employees may receive performance feedback, but it is often informal. "Are you serious? You sent that report?" Most informal feedback is verbal and undocumented. If you want to dismiss or promote your employee, it is crucial that you support your case with as much formal and written documentation as you can.

An opportunity for communication and clarification: Sometimes managers and employees alike are far too busy with day-to-day tasks to properly set and communicate employee expectations. Performance evaluations give employer and employee a chance to compare assignment notes and to prioritize what needs to be done.

HOW TO CONDUCT A GREAT PERFORMANCE REVIEW

Unfortunately, many managers see the performance evaluations as something to get done as quickly as possible—or put off as long as possible. However, when managers are too hasty in their completion of these evaluations, they fail to be thorough in their assessment of employees. The result is inaccurate, incomplete, and meaningless performance feedback. And when this critical management exercise is half-hearted, employees cannot improve in their jobs, and the goals managers set for their organizations may never be completed.

The performance evaluation process goes beyond the more formal, written aspects of it—no need to see evaluations as a boring burden you must get rid of at the end of every quarter or year. Yes, doing performance appraisals is definitely work, but when you do it—and do it well—the payoff can be considerable.

Here are four steps for conducting great performance appraisals:

Step 1: Set standards and goals. After setting goals and expectations with employees, you must have these goals and expectations communicated clearly before employee evaluations, not after. Let them know about standards as soon as they begin employment.

Step 2: Continuously give specific feedback. Feedback is most effective when given regularly. If you see your employees doing something right, let them know then and there. The same goes for if they are doing something wrong. Ultimately, you want to eliminate surprises from formal performance evaluations by giving regular, clear feedback.

Step 3: Prepare written and formal performance evaluations with your employee. The formal performance evaluation should summarize expectations and goals for the employee. To make this a more engaging process, have employees finish their own performance evaluations in parallel with the ones you prepare. Then, in your performance evaluation meeting, discuss the similarities and differences between their comments and yours. When you meet with employees in person to talk about performance evaluations, your workers will appreciate the personal touch.

Step 4: Set new standards and new goals. Performance evaluations give you the chance to review what works and what does not. Based on your findings, you will then be able to set new expectations and goals for the next review period.

Here are some more helpful tips to remember as a manager:

- Eliminate surprises by communicating frequently with employees, especially when it comes to giving them informal feedback.

- Look to the future with your performance appraisal process and be sure to discuss learning and development.

- Focus on looking forward rather than looking back. Emphasize setting new goals and improving future performance, because employees cannot change the past. They can, however, learn from it and improve.

DOING THE RIGHT PREP WORK

Not all employee evaluations are given the time and attention they deserve. In reality, evaluating employee performance is a year-round job, not just a three-page form you fill out once a year. But some managers still fail to write meaningful and insightful evaluations, and other managers transform these important meetings into one-way presentations instead of two-way conversations.

Thus, you must prepare for this important management exercise accordingly. Avoid these very common evaluation mistakes and you will certainly make the most out of performance evaluations, for both you and your employees.

Comparing: An individual employee's performance should be assessed on its own. Be wary of rating two employees simultaneously, for one high-performing employee may make the other employee look low-performing in comparison.

Mirroring: Let's face it. We tend to like those who are most like us. But if you find yourself favoring an employee who has the same interests, hobbies, or dislikes as you, you may give an evaluation that is not as fair as it should be. Make sure you avoid the favoritism that comes with mirroring.

Nice guy/gal: Evaluation season is not an enjoyable time for some managers. Who *enjoys* acknowledging the failings of their employees *and* telling them about these shortcomings? Remember, employees need to hear the good and the bad. Otherwise, they won't improve.

Halo and recency effects: Sometimes an employee can be phenomenal in one performance area, tempting you to ignore the problems they may have in other areas (*halo effect*). On the other hand, you may be tempted to allow one problem area or instance of poor performance to negatively affect how you see an employee's entire performance (*recency effect*). Don't let these effects influence how you evaluate your workers.

4

Back to School: Create a Learning Organization

Success in management requires learning as fast as the world is changing.

—WARREN BENNIS, leadership expert

It's no secret that today's business environment is changing faster than ever. This means that we must learn faster than ever simply to keep up, much less get ahead of all that change. We are living and working in a VUCA world where volatility, uncertainty, complexity, and ambiguity in business reign supreme. If you want to survive and thrive in this environment, then you've got to prime your employees to learn constantly. Not only that, but they must apply what they've learned to solve future problems and challenges and take advantage of opportunities as they present themselves.

What does your organization do with new information? Does it absorb and develop knowledge, putting it to practical use? Or do your employees learn new things one day and forget them the next? As a manager, one of your priorities is to create and lead a *learning organization,* which consistently and effectively applies knowledge to make positive change for the future.

A learning organization is often created in response to the changing business world around it. Because of how unpredictable today's global marketplace is, the smartest companies learn and adapt alongside any changes that are happening. At the same time, changes within an organization happen too. But managers in learning organizations are well aware that changes present huge opportunities, not just issues or challenges.

Leading change is a manager's major focus in a learning organization; reacting to change is an action reserved for more traditional organizations that are less flexible and more static.

Do you want your organization to thrive during today's fast-paced, ever-changing landscape? Design a learning organization by doing the following:

Practice objectivity: During your professional career, no doubt you have come face to face with managers who base all their decisions on emotions. Instead of reviewing facts objectively and working in the best interests of the team, these managers try to please a higher-up with more influence or power, hoping to gain some sort of special treatment. Avoid becoming this type of manager. Instead, practice being objective in your own decision-making process, which encourages your employees to be more objective too. It's for the best.

Create an open environment: How can any organization learn if no employees are comfortable with being honest and transparent? A learning organization is an open organization in which employees feel safe enough to communicate their thoughts and ideas. Any manager who wants to create a successful learning organization must make it a priority to eliminate any fear employees may have when it comes to communicating to you, other managers, or other colleagues.

Reward the right behaviors: This sounds simple, but it is absolutely essential. In order to create an organization that consistently learns, you must reward the employee behaviors you see that align with the aims and goals of a learning organization. This means that if you see employees involving themselves in teams, or practicing objectivity in their thinking, you should encourage these employees to keep doing what they're doing.

SYSTEMS THINKING

Older traditions of management required that problems be solved right when they appeared on the scene. Say, for example, an employee is not performing well. A manager would decide to immediately *fix the problem,* for example, disciplining the employee as soon as possible. In fact, any time an issue came up, a manager would have thought that so long as they fixed problems, all would be well.

Unfortunately, this management style subscribes to a Band-Aid technique—a method that ignores underlying issues and instead values and implements short-term fixes. But managers now know that treating symptoms of company failure will do nothing constructive for solving actual problems. The term *systems thinking* describes this awareness, which is an understanding of how one event or mistake affects the entire organization, not just individuals or departments.

Let's look to management theorist Peter Senge of MIT who made major contributions to the idea of systems thinking and learning organizations. According to Senge, "Leadership in a learning organization starts with the principle of creative tension."[1] Creative tension is the natural result of the gap between our vision of the future and our current reality. This tension creates energy and direction to drive the organization forward.

Peter Senge outlined five things you need to do as a manager if you want to successfully apply systems thinking.

Stop blaming others: Says Senge, ". . . it is poorly designed systems, not incompetent or unmotivated individuals, that cause most organizational problems." The most effective managers don't blame employees . . . they get to the heart of the problem and work to fix the flaws found in organization systems or structure.

Ignore the quick fix: Remember, treating underlying causes of organizational failures must be your main focus. Treating symptoms leads to short-term fixes when you are in need of long-term solutions.

Focus on the greatest gains: Where can you put forth the least amount of effort while also making the most significant improvements? Perhaps the most effective and longest-lasting results you seek come from small tweaks and solutions. Says Senge, "Tackling a difficult problem is often a matter of seeing where the high leverage lies, where a change—with a minimum of effort—would lead to lasting, significant improvement."

Know that incidents aren't isolated: Systems thinking asks that you look at things from a broader perspective and understand that all events and changes are connected. Problems are not isolated. In fact, they have an impact on the whole organization.

Discern between two types of complexity: Systems thinking also deals with the complexity of incidents and actions. *Detail complexity* involves many variables while *dynamic complexity* occurs when the effects of a manager's actions are not readily apparent to employees. According to Senge, "The leverage in most management situations lies in understanding dynamic complexity, not detail complexity."[2]

OBSTACLES TO LEARNING

The road to becoming a business or company that successfully uses new information to make gains during times of rapid change will be full of all sorts of obstacles. Establishing and maintaining a learning organization in particular is not without its challenges, because companies are often very resistant to learning and/or considering new practices. From unnecessary policies and red tape, to employees who would much rather stay comfortable with the status quo, many factors impact how much an organization is able and willing to learn.

But the biggest obstacle to an organization's learning is none of these things. Instead, it is typically the organization's management team.

What usually happens when a large business is in trouble? When the organization faces a crisis, top management team members start to play it safe—trying to avoid being blamed for the crisis and potentially fired. In fact, if you pay attention to popular business journals, it is likely that you read news of CEOs forced to resign when a company faces large-scale, unsolvable problems. The new CEO then removes the remaining executive team members, installing their own select executive team.

This can actually be a good way to force learning on an organization that is reticent to do it voluntarily. Axing the top management team is perhaps one of the fastest ways to get an organization to unlearn bad practices and habits that stifle learning, innovation, and success. This matters because, when organizations are in crisis mode, they must rapidly unlearn bad habits in order to turn things around. However, bad habits are typically engrained in company operations, often encouraged (consciously or otherwise) by acting managers and supervisors. Old habits are not easy to get rid of. If an executive team is afraid to embrace real change for the better, then this team is not capable of leading an organization toward success.

Consider a turning point in the corporate history of computer maker Apple. In 1994, former CEO Michael Spindler was able to boost sales by reducing costs of production, slashing product prices, and laying off 2,000 workers. However, despite making moves that led to a substantial increase in sales, Spindler and his team were not able to pull off the more serious power move of being acquired by a larger company. They tried to sell Apple to major companies like IBM and Hewlett-Packard but were unsuccessful in their efforts. These botched attempts to sell the company concerned investors and corporate buyers. Was Apple actually viable in the long term? As people struggled to answer this question, Apple product orders were delayed or switched out for other personal computer alternatives.

At the same time, Apple cofounder Steve Jobs noticed a distinct change in how the company was establishing its presence in the personal computer market. Apple had previously been able to separate itself from the rest of the available PC options (which were typically less powerful and cheaper) due to its leadership in areas of innovative technology and design aesthetics. But, as Jobs realized, "Apple didn't fail.... We succeeded so well, we got everyone else to dream the same dream.... The trouble is the dream didn't evolve. Apple stopped creating."[3]

Translation? As PC competitors started to emulate Apple's products and technologies, consumers found no justification for paying for Apple's higher prices. The competitive technological advantage Apple had once relished started to disappear.

On January 31, 1996, at a time when the company was in dire need of major change, Apple replaced Spindler with new CEO Gilbert Amelio. Amelio hired a new chief financial officer and a new chief administrative officer, and he created an entirely new position called the Vice President of Internet Platforms, meant to coordinate and implement new internet strategies for Apple. After Amelio cleared out the old executives and hired new ones, Apple was a company transformed, unlearning the bad habits and practices that had previously blocked it from success.

Fortunately, there are other ways to unlearn bad company habits besides letting go of your executive or management team. If you do not want to partake in the sometimes costly and time-consuming process of changing management, create a learning organization instead. In doing so, your employees will learn how to respond and adapt to change, and managers will feel more secure about the stability of their jobs.

STARTING A QUALITY IMPROVEMENT PROGRAM

Selling high-quality products and services is one of the most important things a business can do. Anything less can threaten the long-term health and viability of your organization. Great managers know they may need to initiate a quality improvement program if they want to deliver the highest-quality products and services.

But not all quality improvement programs are created equal. If you want to create a long-lasting and effective quality improvement program, follow these steps before program launch.

Step 1: Get the support of your top managers. Your top management team not only needs to be aware of your quality improvement program, but they also have to actively support and encourage its implementation. Explain to them the benefits of such a program to your company's bottom line.

Step 2: Start a steering committee. Comprised of employees across different departmental lines and levels, this committee establishes the systems and practices meant to get improvement suggestions from employees. The committee then reports improvement recommendations to management.

Step 3: Establish procedures and guidelines. There are many program models to choose from, but in general, they all have the same things in common. All successful quality improvement programs ask for suggestions from employees, review these suggestions for merit, and then implement them, tracking progress along the way. Proper procedures and guidelines help your company get on the right track toward improvement.

Step 4: Keep your employees in the know. When you make a formal announcement about your program to your employees, you are communicating to them that the organization is prioritizing continual improvement. This information also empowers employees, because they learn that they have been given authority to make legitimate organizational changes.

Step 5: Review program results. From time to time, assess employee participation in your program and whether there are still any existing problem areas within the organization. Make sure you also evaluate the time and money saved, the systems improved, and any other improvements generated by your program. This is how you know that you are getting results.

Teamwork Makes the Dream Work

Alone we can do so little;
together we can do so much.

—HELEN KELLER, author

How many decisions do you make in a typical business day as a manager? Two or three? (Doubtful.) Fifteen to twenty-five? (More likely.) More than that? (Certainly possible.) The typical workday for most managers is made up of a series of decisions. Some of these decisions are naturally more important than others.

Depending on what company you work for, the industries and locations in which your company does business, and your position on the organizational chart, you are likely faced with a variety of different decisions each day. These decisions might include choices like how much to budget for a new-product initiative, where to build a new pharmaceutical manufacturing plant, whether to license technology from a third party or allocate precious research and development funds to develop it in house, how annual bonuses will be allocated to deserving employees, what employee work schedules will be like, or the location of next summer's company picnic.

The central function of any business leader—whether a C-level executive, project manager, department head, supervisor, or, increasingly, front-line employee—is to make decisions. It's part of the job description, sometimes explicitly spelled out and sometimes not. In every organization, individual decision makers make hundreds or even thousands of decisions, big and small, each day. Most organizations are pushing the authority to make decisions to an ever-wider group of executives and managers. Decision empowerment works because often the front line has better information and understands the challenges of execution.

However, this empowerment has to be accompanied with training to develop good decision skills. Contrary to the saying, "We all learn from our mistakes," learning only from our own mistakes is much too slow. We have to learn from the mistakes of everyone—and their successes as well—to avoid unnecessary mistakes.

Although the vast majority of specific decisions has a small impact on the business or its people, customers, vendors, or shareholders ("Should I respond to this email message now, or in five minutes?" "Should I have my admin assistant make a copy of this or do it myself?"), collectively, these small decisions define the nature of an organization's culture and ability to perform. Some specific decisions—the strategic decisions—can and do have a dramatic impact, creating turning points that will forever change the destiny of the business and its people in ways that are good, bad, or someplace in between.

You may think that, as a manager, you are responsible for all the decision-making in your department or organization. You're the leader, so you should be calling the shots, right?

Managers are in charge, but *effective* managers know how valuable it is to empower their teams. Many managers feel that *they* are the ones who can best make the decisions that affect a company's customers or products. However, that is not always the case.

When front-line workers and teams have the authority to serve and address the needs of customers, clients are better served. Plus, managers will have more free time to pursue managerial tasks, like long-range planning, coaching, and mentoring.

EMPOWERING YOUR TEAMS

Team empowerment also serves as an incredible booster for morale and productivity. After all, when a manager empowers workers, employees realize they are trusted to make decisions and that they are important to company success. As a result, employees become more engaged in what they do, and company loyalty increases.

Ultimately, a more efficient and more effective organization can be yours if you empower your employee teams. Here's how.

Focus on Quality

Successfully empower your teams by involving them in your organization's quality control process.

In the 1980s, US managers started to take note of successful Japanese businesses, which were highly regarded for their innovative electronic products and high-quality automobiles. These managers found that many Japanese programs empowered workers by encouraging them to make decisions regarding their own work processes. For example, Motorola management allowed self-directed teams to schedule their own work and decide how to be trained.

Operate Small and Keep It Agile

If you are a smaller and more agile competitor, you will have an edge over large organizations in the marketplace. After all, large organizations often have unnecessary communication channels, delays in response time, and other bureaucratic blockages. Make sure your organization has small teams that can make decisions and take action without approval—this will result in better and faster decisions, allowing customers to receive services and products in an efficient manner.

Adapt and Stay Innovative

Because of its size and flexibility, a team can adapt quickly to company or external changes. Plus, with so many individual skills and perspectives joining forces in one group, a team can even bring about increased innovation.

Long gone are the days when teams were useful for just project completion. Instead, teams are now critical for the long-term needs of every organization.

DIFFERENT KINDS OF TEAMS FOR DIFFERENT KINDS OF TASKS

When you're first putting a team together, you need to consider what kind of team you hope to create. There are different kinds of teams for different kinds of assignments or desired outcomes.

Consider the three major team types that follow. Which will need your managerial support, and which type best fits your organization's needs?

Formal

Created to accomplish specific goals, formal teams provide structure for soliciting performance feedback as well as task assignment. Types of formal teams include

Committees: Committees are permanent or long term and they perform specific organizational tasks that have no set end or final time of completion. For example, companies have committees that meet to plan annual conferences or convene to select employees for quarterly performance awards. Committees can have a changing membership roster, but they continue to work from year to year.

Command teams: These hierarchical teams (for example, management teams, executive teams, and so forth) consist of a manager and employees who directly report to that person.

Task forces: If you have specific issues or problems that need to be addressed, then you'll probably want to temporarily assemble a task force. These formal teams typically have deadlines for fixing problems and will report their findings to management. After they report their findings, the teams are typically dissolved.

Informal

Sometimes teams will form spontaneously within your organization without your direct intervention. You may not even be aware of them. If a group of employees eat lunch together every day or hang out with each other during or after work, then an informal team has formed.

Although informal teams haven't actually been assigned certain goals or tasks, these groups are still incredibly important to organizations. Informal teams give employees a safe outlet to vent about issues or to find solutions to problems by way of informal and unconstrained discussion. Even further, informal teams can give employees another way to receive information, outside of formal communications channels.

Self-Managed

Want the best of both worlds? Self-managed teams, under the guidance of management, have attributes of both formal and informal teams. They are comprised of members who accept responsibility for a team's day-to-day operations and are a prime example of when management is willing to give workers more autonomy and authority. Self-managing teams are typically

- Smaller in size, as larger sizes lead to communication problems
- Empowered to act
- Diverse, comprised of members of different departments who bring with them different perspectives

Self-managed teams have the ability to find solutions to common problems among workers and often make major contributions to a company's success.

THE KEYS TO EFFECTIVE TEAMWORK

For teams to do their best work, they must be empowered by a manager and given the authority and autonomy to make decisions that affect the organizations for which they work. But how do you know a manager has actually empowered the employees on a team? When can you be sure you're not seeing a mere imitation of empowerment? Authentically empowered teams usually

- Set commitments and goals
- Add or remove members of the team
- Receive rewards as a team
- Define and perform their training
- Make the most of team decisions

Unfortunately, true empowerment can be a rarity. Because of this, for many teams, there is still plenty of room for improvement. This is particularly the case in the areas of intragroup trust, role and idea conformity, and overall group efficiency. To counter any existing team ineffectiveness, follow these recommendations:

Focus on real empowerment: A study of team leaders, managers, and team members at various companies revealed that real-world teams are more participative than empowered. That is, they participate in team meetings and so forth, but they don't have the authority they need to make important decisions. To counter this, consider doing the following to get the most out of your team dynamic:

- Allow team members to independently make important long-term decisions.
- Allow team members to select leaders.
- Openly advocate for the team.

Set the stage for a more effective team: Although you will step back from the day-to-day running of the team, you can create the conditions for its success:

- Give the team permission to discipline members who perform poorly.
- Be sure team leaders and team members are trained.
- Acknowledge all team and individual contributions.

Eliminate conflict at its source: As a manager, you must be willing to live with the results of the teams you help assemble. Here's how to best accept any outcome:

- Work to unify the views of the manager and team members.
- Acknowledge and work through personality conflicts.
- Provide adequate tools and resources for the entire team.

Team empowerment is not something that just happens out of the blue. If you are making continuous and pointed efforts to make sure teams are given authority and autonomy, you will find a more empowered, productive, and successful team and company in your hands.

THE ART AND SCIENCE OF DOING MEETINGS RIGHT

In a survey some years ago, Microsoft found that people spend 5.6 hours a week in meetings and that 71 percent of American workers said that the meetings they participate in "aren't very productive."[1] That's a problem. Although many employees in meetings are anxiously thinking about that desk full of work they should be doing, others are daydreaming or checking their smartphones for messages.

There are many ways for meetings to go wrong. Despite this, they are a fundamental part of how teams get work done, and they are essential for any organization. The key is to have good meetings, not bad ones.

You might not realize it, but aside from mastering the basic skills of team management, it's imperative that you do the same for meeting management. After all, the members of your team will communicate with each other and conduct business primarily in the meeting forum.

Common Meeting Problems to Avoid

Did you know there is a good chance most of the meetings held in your office have been largely unproductive? According to a study by Accountemps, approximately 25 percent of time spent in meetings is worthless and a waste of time. Couple this percentage with the fact that an estimated 21 percent of working hours are spent in meetings—with upper management spending even more time in them—and you start to see the value of learning and applying effective meeting skills.[2]

But why are so many meetings today going so wrong? Here are some possible reasons:

Meetings last too long: Many managers fill out the allotted meeting time with items irrelevant to the business at hand. Next thing you know, a meeting that could have been wrapped up in just twenty minutes turns into a sixty-minute meeting—simply because a sixty-minute meeting was on the schedule.

Too many meetings are being held: When you're headed into a crunch time, you may need to have a lot of meetings to keep everyone in close communication. However, this is probably not the case when things aren't so hectic. If you're having a lot of meetings and not much is getting done, schedule fewer meetings and see what happens.

Participants are unprepared: If meeting attendees are not adequately prepared beforehand, then they may very well be lost throughout its duration. Ensure that attendees have done their homework before the meeting starts—not after.

Meetings are unfocused: Meetings can lack focus if participants are not prepared and if managers fail to keep meetings on topic. From distractions to personal agendas, there are many ways a meeting can go off track.

Certain participants dominate meetings: Many meeting attendees can feel intimidated by any loud and opinionated team members (there are always one or two). When this happens, the team hears fewer perspectives and critical contributions can be stifled.

KEYS TO A GREAT MEETING

With so many ways for a meeting to go wrong, there are still many steps you can take to make sure the rest of your meetings can go right. Here's how:

Be on time: Punctuality matters. Start and end meetings on time. This sets a good example for participants, it shows you are serious, and it demonstrates that you respect their time.

Focus less on exclusion: Instead of thinking about who you *aren't* going to invite to participate in a meeting, think about who you *are* going to invite. However, make sure that those invited have a good reason to participate.

Be prepared: Don't be that boss who wanders into a meeting unprepared—wasting your time and everyone else's as you try to get up to speed. Be fully prepared before the meeting starts.

Create an agenda: The agenda is critical for a successful meeting. It gives team members advance notice about topics of discussion, providing them with the opportunity to prepare for the meeting ahead of time. This saves time and improves productivity.

Decrease the number of meetings you have: This is really a case where quality counts far more than quantity. Decrease the number of meetings you schedule, but increase the quality of the remaining meetings. Call meetings only when they're necessary. No more, no less.

Document action items: Create a surefire system to document, summarize, and assign action items to individuals after meetings are completed. Flipcharts, apps, digital note taking—these are just a few of the tools you can use to capture action items. If you want your meetings to have purpose and direction, you will have to create task assignments and follow-up actions. Spend less time merely talking and more time doing.

Acquire feedback: How do you know how effective your meetings are unless you hear thoughts from meeting attendees? Find out what you do right and what you need to improve in order to strengthen future meetings.

Don't be afraid to use tools: In today's world, there are so many resources and tools you can use to improve how meetings are held. These include project management tools or even websites that help craft agendas. Plus, if a key member of your team is working remotely, you can use internet voice and video call programs or apps to hold meetings with all invitees. Examples of these include Skype, Zoom, Google Hangouts, or any number of apps included on your iPhone or Android smartphone.

PART II

REALLY KEY NEW BOSS SKILLS

*You gotta build a team that is so talented,
they almost make you uncomfortable.*

—BRIAN CHESKY,
co-founder, Airbnb

Successful managers do what they do by applying specific skills to achieve their goals. The better honed and practiced these skills, the more effective the manager. In this Part, we will explore the skills that managers need to manage well while creating a high-performing organization. Topics include

- Leadership
- Delegation
- Creating a vision and mission
- Coaching and mentoring
- Motivating today's employees

6

Leadership: Inspiring Those Who Work for and with You

A boss has the title, a leader has the people.

—SIMON SINEK, author

When we think of great bosses, we usually think of men and women who are great *leaders*. According to the old saying, there's nothing new under the sun. And although a seemingly endless supply of new leadership books every year might make you think that the theory of and practice of leadership are changing, the truth is, the core of what makes leaders *great* leaders has changed little over the years.

Think for a minute about some of the widely accepted traits of the very best leaders. They are decisive, fair, charismatic, honest, knowledgeable, and trusting, and they are experts at creating a compelling vision of the future. It's hard to imagine that these traits—and others like them—are any different today than they were for great leaders of decades or even centuries past. Human nature is human nature. It hasn't changed all that much since the first humans walked the earth millions of years ago.

As a manager, you are also a leader. Your people look to you for direction and inspiration in their jobs. Your organization looks to you to lead the way. Your community looks to you to set an example for others to follow. The world looks to you to make our planet a better place for all of us to live.

Do your policies and your work environment attract the best and the brightest in your industry? And, just as important, are these employees sufficiently motivated to stay once you've hired them? Are employees a real part of your team? Do you delegate the authority they need to do their jobs— and do you trust them to follow through? Do you make them feel important, and do you reward them when they do a good job?

If you answered no to any of these questions, then you need to work on your leadership skills. So, how can you be a better leader? What does it take? In this chapter, we'll take a close look at one of the most important jobs of any manager: being a leader.

THREE THINGS EVERY GREAT LEADER DOES TODAY

Years ago, management expert James MacGregor Burns wrote, "Leadership is one of the most observed and least understood phenomena on earth."[1] In reality, I personally believe that today, leadership is actually one of the most observed *and* the most understood phenomena on earth. We know what great leadership looks like, we know what it takes to lead, and we know what separates great leaders from bad leaders.

Sometimes it seems like our favorite leaders were born to lead. And although it may be true that some of today's leaders were equipped with innate leadership skills and capabilities, it does not mean leadership is limited to those simply born with it. In fact, *anyone* has the power to learn what a leader does and how to strengthen their leadership skills.

Let's consider three things that every great leader does today.

Creates a Supportive Environment

A workplace that punishes employees for saying what's on their minds, taking risks, and telling the truth is not a productive workplace, and it is certainly not an environment in which workers want to work. Some managers punish their employees for disagreeing with higher-level supervisors, for pointing out mistakes and issues, or even for speaking up. This is a huge mistake for any leader to make. When you intimidate your employees and use fear to try to motivate them, they won't give their very best ideas and efforts to the organization. Instead, they'll do everything they can not to get in trouble.

The very best leaders support their employees and provide them with a culture and environment that encourages safe-to-fail experiments. When their boss has their backs, employees feel secure enough to take chances important for the success of the organization. They might not always succeed—they may even fail. But they learn lessons that advance the organization one more step forward.

Opens Communication Channels

It's essential that every leader communicates well and often with their people. Employees typically want to have a voice in their organizations (who could blame them?) and hope that their suggestions and perspectives are heard by their boss and other leaders. To earn this kind of commitment from your employees, you must communicate with them often, transparently, and sometimes in different ways.

To open communication channels most effectively, managers must first learn to be better communicators. As Gil Amelio, former CEO of Apple, explains:

> *Developing excellent communication skills is absolutely essential to effective leadership. The leader must be able to share knowledge and ideas to transmit a sense of urgency and enthusiasm to others. If a leader can't get a message*

across clearly and motivate others to act on it, then having
a message doesn't even matter.[2]

Great leadership is not a one-way street. Rather, it is a two-way exchange of ideas, where leaders create a vision and goals with their people, and their people communicate their own ideas for how to achieve these goals and vision. The old-style command-and-control model of management no longer works because most employees are not willing to take commands the entire day. If you think effective management and leadership translates to ordering your workers around, you are seriously mistaken.

Inspires and Motivates

The most productive, loyal, and inspired workers are well accustomed to feeling pride in their organization. They believe in the organization and what it stands for, so these workers are more than happy to put in the extra effort for their work to succeed. Although this sounds like an idealistic version of the modern workplace, it is also a reality that many workers still strive to be a part of. It is a highly motivated workplace and an environment in which leaders inspire employees to do their best. As Hewlett-Packard cofounder Bill Hewlett once said, "Men and women want to do a good job, a creative job, and if they are provided the proper environment, they will do so."[3]

In knowing the real value of their employees, a leader can inspire action necessary for company success. Ultimately, a leader uses their knowledge and skills to tap into the untouched well of energy and creativity all employees have.

However, few managers actually reward the workers who are most creative. In fact, many managers might not even recognize when a worker consistently goes above and beyond job expectations because they are too busy searching for workers who do exactly what they are told. This results in a dry, uninspired workplace—one that lacks innovation as well as individual and company direction and progress.

But when a *true* leader leads an organization, worker ideas and motivation rarely go to waste. By clearing obstacles to pride and creativity, and by establishing and nurturing a compelling company vision, true leaders unleash their employees' untapped skills and talents. Employees discover the initiative and energy they might not have known they had, and leaders discover exactly what their employees are capable of accomplishing. Both employees and leaders are often pleasantly surprised with the results.

As a manager, take advantage of the opportunity you have to use your influence for creating energy in the workplace, rather than draining energy with red tape, policies, and bureaucracy. Lead your employees with your vision, and then remove the roadblocks that prevent them from unlocking their full potential. Remember, your vision should be challenging enough to achieve but not so difficult that reaching it is impossible.

FOUR CHARACTERISTICS OF GREAT LEADERS

In today's new workplace environment, the only constant is change. As businesses continue to transform (in every way, at any moment, all the time), great leadership remains dependable and unwavering.

Although faced with unrelenting change, the very best leaders all share a common set of leadership characteristics. As you practice your own leadership skills, be sure that these characteristics are a part of the way you lead.

Great Leaders Are Decisive

A leader has the very important responsibility of making the decisions needed to keep organizations—and the people working for them—moving toward their goals. Although managers are hired to make decisions, it is common for managers to be afraid of making the wrong decisions. As a result, many managers hired to lead their organizations postpone making decisions—often precisely when such decisions are needed most.

Decision skills can be learned, and decision quality can be improved. Centuries of development in the decision sciences—and the last couple of decades of practical application with organizations small and large in many different industries—prove that there is a good way and many wrong ways to make decisions. The key is knowing the fundamental requirements of decision quality and then systematically applying this knowledge in the way you decide. Decision-quality methods have now been honed for a couple of decades. They are widely applied in a few "big-bet" industries like oil and gas and pharma. However, they are still new to most executive decision makers. And even in industries where decision quality is routine in one area, we find decision makers in other areas making the same old mistakes.

Great leaders have the capability to make decisions. Sometimes these decisions need more analysis and deliberation. When that's the case, decisions are made slowly and strategically. In other cases, they can and should be made in a quick fashion. No matter the nature of the decision, the decision is still made. Remember that being decisive is one of your key jobs as a leader—and as a manager.

Great Leaders Have Integrity

Integrity is one of the traits that most employees want from their leaders. When an organization's leaders conduct themselves with *integrity*—with values, ethical behavior, and a sense of fairness—an authentic and positive difference can be made in the lives of many, from customers to employees. When leaders set an example of honesty and integrity for their people to follow, they get the same behavior from their people—developing loyalty and positive feelings for the organization along the way.

A third or more of an employee's waking hours are spent on his or her job. Naturally, people want to spend some of that time making a positive impact on people's lives, whether their organization disposes of harmful chemicals, makes kitchen appliances, or serves sushi. Ultimately, when employees work for an organization that has good values and is led by men and women who value ethics and integrity, they derive remarkably strong internal rewards from their work.

Great Leaders Are Optimistic

Even if a leader faces challenging work and adversity while they pursue the organization's goals, they will always see the future as exciting and brimming with opportunity. Optimistic leaders touch not only employees but also all those who come into contact with these positive people in some way.

In fact, optimism is contagious. After all, who wouldn't want to work for someone who makes them feel good about themselves or their futures? Pessimistic managers hardly sound appealing; their negativity demotivates and drains employees and coworkers alike. Instead, a great leader who is optimistic can transform an organization saturated with naysayers into an organization full of excited, productive workers with higher morale. Lean toward optimism—you will not regret it.

Great Leaders Are Confident

A great leader rarely, if ever, doubts the capabilities of their team. Leaders know their teams can achieve anything they set their minds to, and this confidence motivates these teams toward success. In most organizations, employees mirror the behavior of their leaders. If leaders are confident about the abilities of themselves and the employees who are assigned to their teams, then employees are confident too.

That's why you should avoid acting unsure and hesitant as a leader—your workers will take your cue and be unsure and hesitant as well. Because a confident leader begets confident followers, businesses with a confident leader in charge often achieve a level of success that far exceeds the competition.

So, move forward with confidence. Do your homework and know your stuff. With your experience, your skills, your hard work and talent, it only makes sense that you show the world the confidence you feel deep inside.

GREAT LEADERSHIP BEGINS WITH SELF-LEADERSHIP

I firmly believe that great leadership begins with self-leadership. You can't lead others until you can lead yourself. *Self-leadership* means understanding yourself thoroughly, understanding your own values, and evaluating what's most important to you. As your organization scales, your team should reflect your ethics, values, and beliefs. This all stems from self-leadership.

When you're still the one-person show, you structure your business in whatever way you know how. You build that structure out in your mind initially, and that becomes a framework for the organization as it grows and you hire new people. As you continue to hire, everyone needs to be aligned with your vision and values, which are naturally the vision and values of your organization. New hires may bring different experience and talents to the table, but their values need to be aligned with you as the leader, and they need to reflect that outwardly as you scale growth as one company.

Alan Mulally, former CEO of the Ford Motor Company, had tough calls to make when repairing his company following the automotive industry crisis of 2008–2010. But, throughout, he believed that you should genuinely love your employees and your customers. What makes a great leader different from an ok leader is that they really do care about the day-to-day lives of their people, both their professional and personal success. When it comes to the people with whom you work, this is a case where love is actually not a four-letter word.

Great leaders love the communities in which they do business. They love the world and they want to make it a better place. Take Starbucks and their announcement to ban plastic straws globally by 2020 as an example.[4] The leadership team decided that although the switch might be costly, it's ultimately worth it for the environment, for customers, and for Starbucks' future as a sustainability-focused company.

SHARING LEADERSHIP WITH YOUR PEOPLE

In an increasing number of organizations, leaders are sharing leadership opportunities with employees at all levels, from the front line to every level of employee up through supervisors and managers. When we forego the traditional model of leadership—where one leader has many followers and layer after layer of supervision abounds—we create a more effective form of *collaborative* leadership.

The Orpheus Chamber Orchestra in New York City is one of the rare orchestras that does not have a conductor. Instead of just one leader, every musician in Orpheus has the opportunity to lead—leaders naturally emerge for each piece that the orchestra decides to perform.

To share leadership with your people and create an organization where collaboration is the rule instead of the exception, consider doing what the Orpheus Chamber Orchestra does:

Put power in the hands of the people doing the work: The employees who make the best decisions that directly affect customers are often the ones closest to customers.

Encourage individual responsibility: Make sure those who now have more power also take more responsibility for the quality of their work.

Create clarity of roles: Clearly define roles and responsibilities for employees so they can effectively and comfortably share leadership duties with others.

Share and rotate leadership: When you share and rotate leadership positions, your organization taps every employee's leadership potential—especially if they aren't normally part of the leadership hierarchy.

Foster horizontal teamwork: Horizontal teams, which reach across organizational and department boundaries, are beneficial because they obtain input, make decisions, and help provide answers and solutions.

Learn to listen, learn to talk: Great leaders are active listeners, and they aren't afraid to make their views known to others. Collaborative leadership encourages employees to contribute their opinions and ideas, in addition to listening to others.

Seek consensus: The members of a team or larger organization must be aligned with the organization's mission and agree to move together in the same direction at the same time. If there's deadlock, then a process must be in place to break it.

Dedicate passionately to your mission: One way to involve others in the leadership process is to inspire them to feel passion for their organization. Express passion in your mission and you just might inspire others to care as well. This will positively affect their performance and participation in leadership.[5]

Businesses cannot afford to limit leadership to a few high-level individuals. All employees can take leadership roles by making decisions, serving clients and colleagues, and improving policies and procedures. If your organization gets the most out of every employee through collaborative leadership, your business will not only survive and prosper, but it will always stay ahead of the curve.

THE LEADERSHIP ENVIRONMENT

Current research and examples from real organizations today show us that business and political leaders are again learning, sometimes the hard way, the facts of human nature and the ways toward long-term success. These lessons are described in this book—I explore these strategies, then reinforce them with examples and research from today:

The world is a dangerous place. Any business, no matter how successful, can become extinct (or at least marginalized) rather quickly. Everyone from leaders to front-line employees must be highly attuned to the threats and opportunities that are constantly presented to the organization. Allowing a corporate culture that accepts complacency, hubris, or an internally focused, politically charged atmosphere reduces the power of the enterprise and puts it at risk.

Strong leaders are needed to run an enterprise, but controls are also needed to keep them in check. The same characteristics that make people powerful leaders often pull them too far from the best long-term interests of their enterprise. This feature of human nature is not one that should be judged. Rather, it should be accepted, talked about openly, and managed. The idea of demanding strength in leaders while requiring collaboration and control resonates with us as we see the results achieved by superior CEOs, boards, and management teams.

People at all levels need to be engaged to get the most success from the enterprise. Unfortunately, in most organizations today, they are not. We've all heard of the question: WIIFM, or "What's in it for me?" This is a very important question for each stakeholder in an enterprise. To invest anything—capital, effort, time—we must feel that, ultimately, there will be some benefit to us as individuals. Research today confirms that obtaining the extra incremental effort from each individual can make the difference between marginal performance and great success. This means building business and social practices that maximize the engagement and productivity of the workforce.

External enterprises such as customers, alliance partners, or competitors are all run by people—and so all are subject to human nature. Carefully managing human nature can allow a company to balance competing external forces to great effect. Today's competitive and ever-changing business environment requires complex interrelationships across businesses, as well as a keen focus on customer preferences. Current business leaders with a long-term view must balance the wants and needs of these external parties in ways that are mutually beneficial over time.

Your brand is who you are, not who you say you are. A brand can bring people together internally and represent an enterprise to the world quickly and viscerally, contributing to the success of the enterprise. But in order for it to do that, employees, customers, and partners must experience organizational behavior that complements the brand image, providing that "click of recognition" that says, "Yes, this is real."

Organizational structures cannot either centralize or decentralize; they must allow for both. Management consultants make a fair amount of money helping organizations sort through their decision-making structures. We centralize for a while and then realize that decision-making is too far from the source of business. We decentralize and then realize that we've lost efficiencies and focus. The key is to find balance over time. Certain business-critical issues should be centralized decisions. Why? Because the profitability of the enterprise may be won or lost based on those decisions. Non-business-critical decisions can be decentralized and farmed out to teams of employees. Leaders must recognize that one cannot centralize *or* decentralize— one needs to do both and adjust the balance over time to sustain success.

The world is not static—only those who evolve survive. Leaders must stay true to their core competencies while evolving those skills into more capabilities over time. The best leaders constantly upgrade themselves—not just to survive, but to thrive. Likewise, today's fluid business world requires constant innovation and evolution.

7

Delegation: Making the Most of Your Leadership

Deciding what not to do is as important as deciding what to do.

—JESSICA JACKLEY, entrepreneur and investor

As a manager, you are now obligated to not only grow your current skills and capabilities, but develop new skills in different areas as well. You and your organization will benefit from your analytical, organizational, and even technical skills. But, above all, your people skills will be your saving grace in many managerial situations.

In fact, the ability to delegate well is one of the most critical people skills you'll use on the job and is any manager's number one management tool. An inability to delegate well will most likely make managing a much more difficult task.

Why do managers find it so difficult to successfully delegate? Here are some excuses that managers commonly use for not delegating work, responsibility, and authority to their people:

- "I'm afraid my employees will screw it up."
- "No one can do what I do—as well as I do."

- "I'm just too busy to take the time to delegate."
- "I don't know how to do it."
- "Our customers want *me* to do it."

The best leaders know they can get a lot more done—multiplying their own efforts many times over—when they delegate work to their employees. In fact, a Gallup study of the difference in business performance between organizations whose CEOs had high delegation talent and those whose CEOs had lower delegation talent showed a considerable difference in results. The organizations with high delegation talent CEOs achieved an average three-year growth rate of 1,751 percent—fully 112 percentage points higher than organizations whose CEOs had limited or low delegation talent.[1] That's a remarkable result for something so easy to do.

If you haven't already started delegating work to your people, or you're not convinced you should, here are just some of the advantages:

You can't do everything, all the time: You may be a superstar manager, but everyone hits their breaking point eventually. To shoulder the burden of accomplishing everything for your organization is a noble idea, but in reality, it is simply not possible—especially as your organization and your responsibilities grow. Plus, you need to delegate so you can concentrate on the jobs that only *you* can do, which are often jobs that your staff cannot complete or that are too sensitive for them to work on.

Delegation is an opportunity for employee development: How can your employees take initiative and follow through on tasks successfully if they are never given the chance to do so in the first place? Making decisions and creating ideas are fun and productive things to do as a manager. However, if you never involve your employees and never give them chances to learn new work skills, you end up being stuck doing all the work on your own, since they will not be able to handle it. Plus, today's employees are increasingly reporting that having an opportunity to develop and learn is a top motivator. So, make sure you always give them a chance to grow by delegating important tasks to them.

Delegation increases employee involvement: You don't want robotic employees who act without autonomy, responsibility, or authority. Instead, you want employees who have the ability to independently and effectively carry out tasks. The more you delegate tasks to them, the more likely it is that they will become more involved in day-to-day operations. If you give your employees a chance to thrive, your organization will thrive too.

As a manager, you are responsible for your department's responsibilities. But to personally execute *all* tasks needed for your department to succeed? That's incredibly impractical, and hardly desirable. Delegate, and reap the rewards.

HOW TO DELEGATE

Delegation means putting your faith and trust in another person, whether that be an employee or a colleague. If that individual does not succeed, you are responsible for the outcome. Ultimately, you cannot abdicate your own responsibility for the task until it has been successfully completed. If your employee drops the ball, your boss will still find you at fault, regardless of why the task wasn't completed.

When you understand the strengths and weaknesses of your employees, you will find more success with the delegation process. As you perform your managerial duties, you have to continually work at improving how you delegate. But delegation benefits both managers and employees when done properly. Here's a guide on to how to delegate work to employees effectively and well:

Step 1: Communicate what you want done. All tasks should be properly communicated. Let your employees know what you want completed, when you would like it completed, and what results you are expecting.

Step 2: Give context. To underline the importance of a task, explain why it needs completion, how it fits into the big picture, and what challenges can arise during its performance.

Step 3: Agree on standards. Determine which standards will be used to measure the success of task completion. Make sure standards are reachable and realistic.

Step 4: Give authority. Employees must be given authority to complete tasks, especially without obstacles from coworkers or other roadblocks.

Step 5: Give support. Successful task completion requires training, money, progress check-ins, or other important resources. Support your employees!

Step 6: Acquire a commitment. You want to ensure that your employee has agreed to complete the task. Confirm your expectations and your employee's understanding of what they have agreed to do.

DISCERNING WHAT TO DELEGATE

It is true that you can, in theory, delegate to your employees anything you are responsible for. But if you assign all of your duties to someone else, why would you even be working in your position? The reality is that some tasks are most appropriate for you, the manager, to do, whereas others can be delegated to your people.

Delegate higher-level tasks to your employees as they gain more experience, expertise, and confidence over time. Evaluate how capable an employee is, then assign tasks that meet or exceed their level of expertise; use schedules, and monitor their progress along the way. This helps you see if your employee is being challenged or if they are suitable for the jobs you have given them. The more you delegate, the better you'll get at it.

Still not sure what to delegate? Try assigning the following to employees:

Repetitive tasks: Routine tasks like weekly expenditure reports or monthly budget reviews are a few repetitive tasks you can assign to employees. Your time is focused on higher-level assignments—don't waste it on tasks like these.

Information gathering and detail work: Detailed technical tasks or thorough research can cost you valuable time. Your position as manager requires that you focus on the bigger picture for your team's success. Leave the details and minutia to your employees and concentrate your own efforts elsewhere.

Surrogate roles: As a manager, your presence will be requested for meetings, presentations, and more. However, because you cannot be everywhere at once, give your employees the chance to fill in. This way, you save time, and your employees bring you the most important information from what you missed.

Future tasks: Delegation also serves as a great way to train your staff for future job responsibilities—allowing your employees to assist you in certain tasks gives them a taste of the things they can learn and later take over.

At the same time, there are certain tasks you should not delegate—period. Avoid delegating the following work because these tasks are an integral part of your responsibilities as a manager:

Giving performance feedback: Sure, lower-level employees can praise the work of their colleagues, but formal performance feedback is an official process that requires your involvement.

Creating a vision and goals: As a manager, you hold a unique perspective on the needs of the organization. After all, the higher up the organization you are, the broader your perspective is going to be. Any employee can and should make suggestions and provide input, but it is your job to develop and decide on the organization's long-term vision and goals.

Counseling and discipline: Business today can be busy and hectic, but discipline and counseling are two things that you'll need to do as a manager. Set goals and standards with your people, then counsel them if they can't meet them on your agreed schedule. Know that only you decide if your workers have met expectations or not.

FOLLOWING THROUGH ON YOUR DELEGATION

Picture this: the initial hurdles of delegation have now been worked through. You have assigned your employee a task, and now you wait with anticipation to see the results of their performance. Your employee was given adequate resources and training, and the scope of the task was defined. After telling your employee what results you expect (and when you expect them), what is your next step?

One possible course of action could be checking on the assignment's progress over and over, more frequently as the deadline approaches. You could press your employee for details, thus distracting them from the task at hand and increasing their frustration over your micromanagement. The results may be submitted on time, but they may be incomplete or incorrect, and your employee may be irritated with your apparent lack of confidence in their abilities.

Or you could do absolutely nothing after you assign the task to your employee. Instead of badgering your employee for progress updates or constantly offering support, you put your focus elsewhere. When the deadline arrives, you are surprised to learn the task has not been completed.

Based on these two extreme options, we can see that effectively monitoring the delegation process is absolutely critical for task success. Monitoring styles may differ from employee to employee, but effectively monitoring delegation always requires the following:

Communication lines are kept open: Before it's too late, make sure your employees know and understand that they should let you know if they cannot overcome a problem. Find out if they need more resources or better training, and take time for employees when they request your help.

Track the assignments you make: Whether it's with a calendar, smartphone app, or online project management tools, you need to keep track of basic task assignment details, such as what the task is, who is responsible for its completion, and when it is due. Get organized and success will follow.

Tailor your monitoring approach: Adapt how you monitor employee progress depending on each employee's specific skills and experience. For example, if one employee usually performs their job with little supervision on your part, you can create a monitoring system that has few checkpoints along the way. An employee who needs more support can be monitored with an increased number of checkpoints.

Follow through on agreements: Accountability is key. If reports are late, hold your workers accountable—no matter how tempting it is to let failures slide. Your employees should understand how important it is to take personal responsibility for their work performance, and if you don't communicate this to them, then they might miss deadlines, negatively affecting team goals and successes.

Reward successes and counsel everything else: Let your employees know when your expectations are being met, and when they are not. After all, this is how your teams and organizations know which performances are good and which are bad. And knowledge like this can help secure effective and successful performances for the future. Always remember: criticize in private and praise in public.

8

The Vision Thing

Mission is the star we steer by.
Everything begins with mission,
everything flows from mission.

—FRANCES HESSELBEIN, former CEO, Girl Scouts

When a manager hopes to improve engagement among employees, the first step often involves creating and giving workers a clear and compelling vision for their organization. Employees need to know what exactly it is that the organization is trying to do because this knowledge gives them the motivation to achieve (particularly during work challenges or obstacles). When employees understand the purpose behind tasks, there's a good chance they will more effectively set sail toward individual and team success.

When are employee levels of engagement the highest? When company or personal goals are achieved or surpassed. And as this happens, those who are performing well feel confident, and this positive energy affects and benefits other areas of performance. As an increasing number of employees become motivated and engaged in their jobs, and the more goals are achieved, you may find quality increasing when it comes to products made or the customer service your organization offers.

Customers, impressed by the services they receive, will become more loyal to your brand or company, and sales and revenue can skyrocket. Let's take a closer look at creating a vision and organizational mission.

IT ALL BEGINS WITH VISION

How positive are you that your workers understand the purpose of your organization—its *why*? Try directly checking in with them to find out. Ask employees what they think the mission of the organization is, and what they think their role is (or should be) in achieving this purpose.

If you get the same answers from each person you ask, there's a good chance that the company is on track and all employees have reached a mutual understanding of the group's mission. However, if you receive drastically different answers, you may have to face the facts—your organization's message is unclear, misunderstood, or has changed from what you originally set it out to be.

If your organization's mission lacks clarity, you may use this as an opportunity to revisit the function and purpose of your business or group. Some years ago, I was asked by Frances Hesselbein—chairman of the Frances Hesselbein Leadership Forum and former CEO of the Girl Scouts of the USA—to update a book by management guru Peter Drucker. The book—*The Five Most Important Questions You Will Ever Ask About Your Organization*—is a terrific guide for clarifying an organization's mission.

Here are Peter Drucker's five most important questions:

Question 1: What is our mission? Peter Drucker sums up what a mission is in a very concise way: "The effective mission statement is short and sharply focused. It should fit on a T-shirt. The mission says why you do what you do, not the means by which you do it."

Question 2: Who is our customer? Says Drucker, "Answering the question Who is our customer? provides the basis for determining what customers value, defining your results, and developing the plan."

Question 3: What does the customer value? According to Peter Drucker, "The question What do customers value?—what satisfies their needs, wants, and aspirations—is so complicated that it can only be answered by customers themselves . . . What does the customer value? may be the most important question. Yet it is the one least often asked."

Question 4: What are our results? As Drucker explains, "Progress and achievement can be appraised in qualitative and quantitative terms. These two types of measures are interwoven—they shed light on one another—and both are necessary to illuminate in what ways and to what extent lives are being changed."

Question 5: What is our plan? Plans are important too. Drucker says, "A plan . . . is a concise summation of the organization's purpose and future direction. The plan encompasses mission, vision, goals, objectives, action steps, a budget, and appraisal."[1]

As you start to decide what your teams, departments, or organization should concentrate on in order to be successful, consider beginning this process with some vision clarification. When you get your results, note that they should include a purpose that compels, or a mission that inspires, all involved to pursue new heights. Then, from this vision, you can discern and develop what kind of unique advantages your company has over the competition—what can you offer potential clients that competing organizations cannot?

Your strengths are your advantages in the marketplace; these are the areas that can help you succeed should you capitalize on them. Since the business environment continues to change, you need to stand out more than ever in order to attract and maintain customer attention. The unique competitive advantages you have to offer must be looked at and assessed frequently, because the needs of your customers will shift rapidly and often.

What is currently working for your business and what isn't? This is the question you must ask after you have clarified your group's vision and reevaluated your goals. For example, your longstanding clients may have decided to use your services less frequently, whereas new customers have begun signing up for what you have to offer. Can you determine what your new customers all have in common, and can you use this information to approach similar potential clients?

Your company's goals will require modified strategies as the times change in the modern marketplace. When you need help with these changes, it is a great idea to engage your employees and ask for their ideas and input. Not only will this help your employees feel valuable and give them chances to participate and grow, but you may gain new and improved strategies for better business operations, increased customer service, and smarter fiscal decisions.

COMMUNICATING YOUR VISION AND MISSION

Employees want to know a lot of information during the course of their jobs. They want to obtain all the necessary information they need to complete the tasks they have been assigned, and they want to know how successful the organization is (or isn't) and what coworkers are doing. Topics of interest might include company products and services, success strategies, values and vision, and even current happenings from competing businesses. This may be a lot of information to absorb, but it is the role of management to communicate all of this to employees clearly and effectively.

A large majority of employees want managers to communicate more—and more effectively. Unfortunately, many employees report not getting the communication they need. According to an Interact/Harris poll, 91 percent of employees surveyed say that their managers do not communicate well. More specifically, 57 percent reported that their manager doesn't give clear directions, 52 percent said that their manager doesn't have time to meet with them, and 51 percent reported that their manager refuses to talk to subordinates.[2]

The more effective the communication, the higher the morale. The less effective the communication, the lower the morale. We can be sure about one thing: if an employee is not well-informed, their capacity to perform in the workplace is certainly limited.

Unfortunately, not sharing information with employees is an error many managers and organizations commonly make. For example, high-level management may not share information because they may not be completely certain of what's happening next in a changing business landscape. In other situations, a manager might not share information because they believe sharing information with lower-level staff leads to a decrease in their own status and power.

Sometimes managers have good intentions when they withhold information. However, failing to communicate information can still backfire, no matter the original intention. For example, when management does not tell employees about pending crises or even potential job loss, they may be trying to "protect" their workers. A manager may think that if they don't tell employees this critical news, they are preventing employees from feeling the fear and anxiety associated with it. But more often than not, these well-intended actions lead to secretive hallway conversations and closed-door meetings among management personnel, instilling a sense of unease in employees. And when employees feel uneasy, they only imagine the worst-case scenarios, start to speculate, and feel increased fear.

Employees not only want to know what is happening within their jobs and organization, but they *need* to know news and updates, even if said news is bad and possibly anxiety inducing. If the firm is struggling, there is absolutely nothing wrong with being honest and transparent with those who work for you. In fact, as you communicate more information to your workers, there can even be an increase in teamwork, loyalty, and dedication. You can even use any bad news as a chance to brainstorm with employees about ideas, plans, and solutions.

Bringing your employees into the loop may make you hesitant at first, especially if you think doing so will somehow harm or scare them. However, involving and communicating to employees early and often actually instills in them an increased sense of responsibility, value, and trust.

HOW TO USE DIRECT, TWO-WAY COMMUNICATION

There is no need to sugarcoat how you deliver information that needs to be communicated. In reality, employees aren't looking for a sugarcoated delivery—they're looking for the truth, communicated in a concise and clear manner.

If the company's sales are down, every employee deserves to know. As you communicate and share this information, you emphasize to all employees that the performance of your organization is collectively owned. No matter the level of employment—from front-line staff to executive management—everyone shares responsibility for the organization's performance: revenue, future, and failures included.

The messages you send when sharing important information with employees are not limited to messages merely related to news and updates. When you give your employees behind-the-scenes access to your organization's fiscal landscape and plans, you are sending the underlying message to each of them that they are valuable and critical to your organization's success. This message then creates an increased sense of responsibility and accountability—the employees recognize that rather than the problem, they are part of the solution. A realization like this gives employees the confidence they need to trust in their capabilities, to focus, and to do the work that will help take your organization out of a predicament.

Creating more open lines of communication across your organization can help start a new era of honesty, responsibility, and trust. At the same time, establishing open communication can put an end to certain negative practices, namely gossip and false rumors. Since rumors often arise in uncertainty, and are blanketed in negativity, it's in everyone's interest that you stop them immediately, especially at their source.

When in doubt, err on the side of oversharing information with your people instead of undersharing it. The more certainty you can create within your organization, the less uncertainty there will be, and the less reason for people to gossip or spread rumors. In addition, with better information, workers will be able to make better and more well-informed decisions—successfully moving your organization forward.

TWENTY-FIRST-CENTURY WORKFORCE STRATEGIES

As we look to the future, some common themes are worth considering for success in the coming decades. As you review the themes that follow, consider how they could or should be made a part of your own plans going forward.

Hiring

Gone are the days of throwing people at a problem. As the supply of talented workers tightens, it's more important than ever to hire wisely and to find the very best people for every job in the organization. This requires creating a robust recruitment system that identifies the best candidates, encourages them to apply for open positions, then puts them through a rigorous evaluation and interview process.

At the same time, some managers are completely reinventing their business models or creating new ventures that require fewer employees. Some are reengineering their businesses to create jobs that will take advantage of the skills and attitudes of the achievers in the available talent pool. Nearly all are reevaluating the competency and commitment level of their current workforce.

Every business needs a systematic process for rating employee performance and cutting out the underperformers. This process must be fair and transparent, and it must be unfailingly applied with its results quickly acted upon.

Compensation

Business leaders across the board are looking to shave costs and reduce their payrolls. However most understand that there is a thin line between saving money and creating an unmotivated pool of employees—many of whom are constantly on the lookout for a better paying job in a different company. Attracting the very best talent requires not just paying your employees fairly, but slightly more than the standard market rate for positions in your industry and geographic area. By paying a little more, you'll attract better employees and keep them happier and more engaged in their work.

Ownership

Executives may decide to use stock and ownership as a carrot, but it shouldn't be easily or arbitrarily distributed. Privately held companies are less inclined to give ownership, even to senior employees, if they don't demonstrate specific contributions beyond their salaried objectives. For example, years ago I was granted stock options by a software development company I worked for when I successfully landed and then grew a very large, multiyear contract with one of our customers. I would not have been offered the stock if I hadn't made this major contribution to the company's long-term success. It was well above and beyond my job description at the time.

Culture

It is widely agreed that the focus of company culture should be on creating an environment that encourages employee happiness, inclusiveness, engagement, productivity, and creativity. The need to be agile is enhanced by the strong need for openness, with an emphasis on a powerful collaborative environment in which all are actively encouraged to work together toward a common goal.

Some executives and managers are taking a less traditional angle toward stating common objectives. Rather than looking at size or productivity as the primary objective, Lisa Hendrickson, the owner and COO of multimillion-dollar Hendrickson Custom Cabinetry in New York City, looked closely at company culture. As a result, she restructured her staff into two types of positions: sales and those who support sales. She reconciles quality control and productivity as support components that ultimately increase sales while securing growth and success.

Retention

Business leaders are beginning to explore creative ways to help employees further their personal development in ways that connect them to the company's long-term objectives. This is a crucial point future leaders in management need to keep in mind—not only to reduce the costs of replacing employees, but to ensure their happiness and full engagement in their work. The goal is to ensure that creative and productive employees stay loyal to their organizations and don't leave to work elsewhere. By providing employees with opportunities for growth in-house and a clear path toward such opportunities, managers can, in many cases, postpone employees' exploration of outside opportunities—perhaps indefinitely.

Communication

It is vital for communication channels to be widely available in organizations today to enable fast, easy, and widespread messaging and collaboration between and among employees and management. To accomplish this goal, companies are enhancing and refining their communications systems to create easier alignment among employees and management alike. Cloud-based communication and collaboration systems such as Slack, Trello, Microsoft Teams, and others are gaining a significant foothold in many organizations. In addition, lateral collaborative methods are widely supported now rather than the top-down systems of the past. With more of the decision-making capability falling to the individual performer, meetings are now looked at as opportunities for creative collaboration and for learning how to use each other as resources.

YOUR MANAGER PERSONALITY

Maritz, founded in 1894, designs and runs employee recognition and rewards programs for other companies. When he was an executive with the company, Rick Garlick wrote an article that described six distinct supervisor personality types that emerged from a survey of working Americans conducted by Maritz. These personality types—which are also applicable to managers—determine, to a great degree, how someone manages others and whether they will be rated as a good or bad boss.

Which of these personality types would your employees say *you* bring with you to the office each day?

The respected professional. These managers—who comprise 29 percent of the total in the Maritz survey—conduct business operations efficiently. They are task-driven and are flexible when that's what is required to get the job done. They are honest and reliable, but they maintain a professional distance. Respected professionals are viewed positively by those who work for them. In fact, 76 percent of people surveyed described respective professionals as "Superman or Wonder Woman—open to your ideas."

The caring mentor. These managers are honest, cheerful, generous, friendly, and flexible—and they earn the highest scores when it comes to the engagement levels of their employees. Caring mentors put their employees first and genuinely care about the people who work for them.

Employees with caring mentor bosses—only 26 percent of the total group surveyed—have a stronger affinity toward customers and are more likely to stay with the company for the long term and recommend it to others. Caring mentors were described as Superman/Wonder Woman by 81 percent of survey respondents.

Win-at-any-cost. These managers are considered tough, controlling, inconsistent, clueless, and ruthless, and they are not seen as ethical, honest, or intelligent. In fact, they are often described as *Machiavellian,* that is, they believe that the ends nearly always justify the means. Win-at-any-cost managers are not respected by their employees, and these employees have particularly low engagement scores. Nineteen percent of those surveyed report having bosses like this, and 71 percent said they would fire this person if they could.

The taskmaster. Although—like win-at-any-cost managers—taskmasters are seen as tough and controlling, they score higher in both ethics and competence. Taskmasters have the classic Type A personality, they are focused on achieving their goals and are not cheerful or peaceful. People aren't a priority for taskmaster managers, which results in their employees having fairly low levels of engagement and loyalty. About 10 percent of employees report having taskmasters as bosses, and they generally do not consider these men and women to be effective.

The likeable loser. These managers—comprising 9 percent of the total—may be charming and wholesome, but they are considered incompetent and inconsistent by their employees. Employees do not respect likeable loser bosses and would prefer to have a different boss. Likeable losers were described by survey respondents as The Invisible Man (34 percent) or Charlie Brown (27 percent).

The glad hander. On the surface, these managers seem to be friendly and flexible—a friendlier version of the win-at-any-cost manager. But peel away this façade, and you'll find that glad handers are considered by their employees to be dishonest, unreliable, clueless, and uncaring. The second-worst kind of manager in the survey, about 7 percent of employees reported that they had glad handers as bosses.[3]

TWENTY-FIRST-CENTURY WORKFORCE TACTICS

Here are five action steps you can take to enhance your workforce environment in the current, fast-changing, business environment.

Embrace the cultures. Commit time and energy to understanding the cultural backgrounds of your people. And not just their ethnic or social backgrounds, but how they fit into the workplace. For example, your longtime employees (who may be uncomfortable dealing with fear and change) may not mix well with brand-new employees (who may be highly charged, eager, and empowered), creating conflict and challenge. Management must devote resources to learning about the perspectives of different organizational groups and create cross-cultural programs to nurture empathy across the board.

Adopt open-book management. Those companies still operating their finances behind closed doors will have difficulty maintaining trust and respect among their employees. The only sure way to keep employees from undeservedly wanting what they don't have is to educate them on the realities of the risk and reward. Those who desire both will step up and make the decisions to warrant a piece of the pie.

Create a level playing field with compensation. Avoiding uncomfortable discussions with employees who are being overpaid for underperforming will only exacerbate personnel issues once the truly motivated come to town. The greater external restructuring gives you the opportunity to reexamine and restructure all compensation programs to prepare for employees who are pay-for-performance ready.

Design an internal entrepreneurial program. Many businesspeople want employees who are more entrepreneurial, but they don't foster the personal growth necessary to retain them. Apportion resources to employees who can generate ideas and execute on them. Devise compensation that gives them ownership for what they create. Make sure they are prepared to embrace the full positive and negative impact of true cause and effect as well as total accountability.

Embrace communication technology. Social networking tools are largely used to generate external business, but there is great value to be had with internal application. Younger employees have already been trained in their use. Giving young employees the opportunity to bring older workers on board will elevate their position, allowing them to contribute while empowering your entire workforce to make the most of twenty-first century advances to come.

9

Be a Better Coach and Mentor

Make sure that team members know they are working with you, not for you.

—JOHN WOODEN, basketball coach

The list is never ending when it comes to why you should help your employees improve and develop themselves. From a business standpoint in particular, doing so increases the quality of their job performance. What's also important is that, as a manager, you are in the best position to support employees so they can develop themselves and benefit your organization. From on-the-job learning opportunities and mentoring, to tasks and assignments, the training, development, and guidance a manager offers is unique and critical for employee development.

Still not sure that employee development should be a priority? Here are a few highlighted reasons (among many) that should convince you.

You can give them learning opportunities: Do some of your employees continually make mistakes on assignments? Even if the task appears easy to execute, it is possible that your employees lack the knowledge on how to perform the assignment in question. Your employees may not be incompetent—they may just need someone like you to provide them with guidance, support, and learning opportunities.

You will need someone to take over: Whether it's for the long term, or very briefly, there will be a time when you need someone to step in to take over your high-level duties while you attend to other matters. Prepare your employees accordingly so your organization can still move forward in your absence.

Better employees work smarter: Why would you turn down the opportunity to develop your employees if it means helping them work more effectively and strategically? Find out what your employees have yet to learn about their jobs and responsibilities, then make a concerted effort to give them the support and information they need.

Your employees will appreciate challenges: Some employees are stuck in dull office settings where everything remains the same every day. This leads to decreased energy, motivation, and productivity in the workplace. But if you prioritize developing your employees, any challenges they face in the process will stimulate and motivate them.

Your employees are worth it: If anything, you must develop your employees because new employees cost a lot of time and money to recruit and train. Invest in your employees today so you don't have to waste time and money on replacements tomorrow!

How can you possibly lose if your employees win? When properly and successfully developed, your employees gain high-level skills and capabilities that will, in turn, bring incredible value to your company.

HOW TO DEVELOP YOUR PEOPLE

Employee development is a deliberate, continuous process that requires managers to support their employees. If either managers or employees lose focus during this process, employees won't develop and the organization will have to endure hardships brought by its underdeveloped workers. As a manager, work with your employees to identify areas of improvement, implement development opportunities, and provide resources and support so the needs of your organization can be met.

Consider the following steps to develop employees in order to meet your organization's future challenges:

Step 1: Schedule a meeting with your employee. After assessing your employee's performance, meet with them to discuss your vision for them, as well as where they hope to go in the organization.

Step 2: Have conversations about strengths and weaknesses. Next, have an honest discussion about employee strengths and weaknesses. Identify the areas they can develop to meet challenges and move forward in the company.

Step 3: Assess the present. Determine the current state of your employee's talents and skills and see where they show potential.

Step 4: Create a career development plan. Outline what formal support you can give your employee to develop their skills and detail scheduled milestones.

Step 5: Ensure both parties follow through. Honor your agreement to provide your employee with the support he or she needs, and check on progress regularly.

CREATING PLANS FOR CAREER DEVELOPMENT

Career development plans can be thorough and detailed, but at their core, they must contain these key elements:

Learning goals that are specific: Identify specific learning goals when meeting with an employee to talk career development and planning. No matter the level of employment or experience, all individuals in your organization can benefit from having these types of goals—we all have room to improve.

Goal resources: Once you have discussed learning goals, identify and provide the resources that are required to support your employee with their objectives. These resources can include team assignments, formal training, job shadowing, and more.

Employee resources and responsibilities: Both manager and employee are responsible for an employee's career development. Although a company can pay for training and other development opportunities, an employee should still work on their career in their free time!

Deadlines for learning goals: If goal accomplishment milestones aren't scheduled, how can a career development plan ever be effective? The best goal schedules give employees flexibility as well as enough time for daily tasks and career development progress.

Progress measurement standards: For every goal, be sure to have a clear method for measuring goal completion.

HOW TO BE A GREAT COACH

Critical to an employee's learning process is coaching, which is instrumental for developing self-confidence, acquiring new skills, and learning new things. Anyone can be a good coach—even you, as a manager.

You may be getting familiar with the roles of a manager, but did you know being a coach means being a counselor, colleague, and cheerleader, all at the same time? Much like other business skills, you can always practice and improve the traits a good coach has. Which ones are you employing right now, and which need more work?

Giving support and encouragement: There are many opportunities for new and veteran employees to feel discouraged on the job. A coach knows how to step in and help inspire everyone to get them back on task.

Emphasizing team success: Rather than growing one team member in particular, a coach knows that a team's overall performance is most important. This requires the efforts of every team member.

Inspiring team members: Coaches are especially skilled at inspiring others to do their best and achieve team success.

Creating supportive environments: A great coach knows the importance of a workplace environment that fosters growth and allows success.

Providing feedback: Coaches provide continual and consistent feedback that help employees know what they're doing right and what they're doing wrong. At the same time, employees must let coaches know when help is needed.

Coaching is an activity that requires paying close attention to your employees' specific needs, weaknesses, and strengths. The support you give will vary between team members. Employees who are more independent will require fewer progress checks, and those workers who need help will necessitate a higher level of support.

No matter your coaching style, here are the techniques the best coaches use to elicit stellar performances from their employees.

Explaining the "why": Coaches don't just tell employees what to do, they tell them *why* they're doing it. The most effective coaches always provide big-picture perspective and context for workers.

Being available for employees: Keep your door open to your employees, walk through your office, and always make an effort to visit them at their desks. Doing this lets employees know you are available. In this way, they know who to go to for their needs.

Being a sounding board: Are your employees finding themselves in a predicament? Coaches help employees work through issues by using active listening skills and talking through new ideas and approaches with employees.

Offering help: Workloads can be overwhelming, especially for employees who are just learning their new jobs. Coaches help employees work through transitional phases by taking measures to relieve the pressure, like reassigning current duties to other employees.

Transferring knowledge: Another way coaches help is by giving their personal knowledge and perspective to employees in response to the unique needs of each team member. Coaches have faced many situations during their tenure, and their experiences can help newer employees.

Showing, not just telling: There is no better way of teaching and learning than this method. Lead your workers through work processes by explaining procedures while performing a task, by having them complete the same procedure while you explain steps, and then by having them explain steps while they perform the task again.

An overwhelming majority of your job as a manager consists of building a foundation of small successes every day that will lead to larger victories in the future. Coaches, on the other hand, focus their daily energy on assessing employee progress and seeing how worker strengths, opportunities, and turning points can be capitalized.

You can follow a number of guidelines to handle any employee concern. These include openly giving positive feedback, having relaxed discussions about concerns and areas of improvement, lending a listening ear, and following through with check-ins and support. Make sure you are patient, and express enthusiasm about your confidence in your employee, as well. They will appreciate it and can use this boost to perform well.

THE POWER OF MENTORSHIP

When you're a new employee lacking experience, having someone with experience to help guide you as you work your way up is absolutely invaluable. This person knows how to get to the top, can advise on decisions, and can even act as a coach or sounding board. This person is a *mentor*.

A manager is not always supposed to be a mentor. Although a manager's job is to coach and guide employees, mentors take on a confidential adviser role, and are usually high up in the organization—not the boss of a mentee.

If a mentor has found you, celebrate! A mentor can be a real benefit to you and your organization. Here's why:

Mentors provide experiences with which to grow: Formal career development often requires supplemental activities or training (for example, learning public speaking skills) that you may not know about. A mentor will guide you toward these activities because they are important to your future career growth.

Mentors provide career guidance: Over the years, your mentor has probably seen a number of employees and careers come and go. They have more insight as to which paths in your organization lack value and which provide quick and secure advancement.

Mentors explain the inner workings of an organization: Ever notice the difference between what really goes on in an organization and what is officially announced to employees? Mentors can communicate intimate knowledge and details so you can find out what is actually happening.

Mentors teach by example: Watch and learn. Because your mentor has already seen it all, let them help you learn the most efficient ways to accomplish tasks.

The mentoring process begins when a highly experienced employee recognizes the potential of a new or inexperienced employee. Employees can engage the interest of a potential mentor during project collaboration or when seeking advice, as well.

10

Motivating
Today's Employees

You get what you reward.

—DR. BOB NELSON, motivation expert

Believe it or not, what the typical manager *thinks* their employees desire from their boss and their organization is dramatically different from what employees *actually* want. For instance, showing your appreciation for employees with monetary incentives is actually less motivating than you would expect. Overall, employees report that they rarely receive verbal praise or written thank-yous. This provides you with a golden opportunity to thank your employees for a job well done.

What motivates employees the most? According to reports, manager-initiated incentives (which involve a supervisor or manager giving direct recognition) and incentives based on performance are most valuable to them.

As a manager, you, rather than your organization, should initiate incentives in order for recognition to be most meaningful. These moments of recognition should be regular and frequent, and they should emphasize stellar job performance rather than mere participation.

The following incentives, although simple to execute, are most impactful for employees:

- Offering flexible working hours or time off
- Publicly acknowledging, recognizing, or rewarding employees, in settings like staff meetings or company newsletters; celebrating department and company successes, too
- Involving employees in decision making, allowing for commitment and ownership
- Providing employees with opportunities to hone new skills, and supporting employee goals in an open and trusting work environment
- Frequently giving employees personal or written thank-yous for great job performance

ESTABLISHING A SUPPORTIVE WORK ENVIRONMENT

Even though there are a number of known, effective ways to spur employee motivation, an accelerating and evolving workplace makes it difficult for managers to keep up with employees' wants and needs. But managers who inspire know how to embrace changing trends and business forces.

Under mounting pressure, the best managers use the power of ideas over the power of their positions to motivate employees. They know that threats and intimidation are ineffective ways to motivate higher levels of performance from their people. Want to create a supportive workplace? Here's how.

Make employees feel comfortable and safe. Do your employees have trouble telling you bad news? If so, they don't feel safe enough to communicate their mistakes or concerns. We all make mistakes. Avoid punishing employees for the mistakes they make. Instead, create a safe environment for motivated employees who want to take chances.

Build mutual trust. Increase employee loyalty, morale, and commitment by including your employees, as well as trusting and respecting them. This will result in better ideas as employee motivation improves.

Keep communication open. What gives you an edge over your competition? Quick, efficient, and honest employee communication. A collaborative (not a closed-off) environment fosters team engagement and success.

Remember, your greatest asset is your employees. Management now is less about telling people what to do and more about developing employees. When you challenge and motivate your people, you end up seeing all the positive progress employees make with their successes.

KNOWING YOUR ROLE AS A MOTIVATING FORCE

If you believe as a manager that employees determine how motivated they are, or if certain employees naturally have good or bad attitudes, you may be surprised by how much influence you actually have over employees and how motivated they are. Your managerial duties require you to create a supportive environment that fosters employee motivation, so you should know that *you* determine how unmotivated or motivated your employees are.

So how can you bring out employee motivation? Consider holding your employees to high standards. When you express that you have high expectations for their abilities, your employees will understand that ultimately, you believe in their potential. Soon, they will believe in it, too.

At the same time, you can also give employees the benefit of the doubt in your efforts to motivate them. Instead of reprimands and punishment, consider utilizing training, support, and encouragement as you work to figure out how you can assist with employee success. These suggestions not only help you find the positive in your employees, but they effectively reinforce the behaviors you hope to see in the workplace.

THE LIMITATIONS OF MONEY AS A MOTIVATING FORCE

Although money does make the world go 'round, it certainly isn't everything. It does have some motivational value, but the reality is, it isn't the strongest factor of an employee's job performance. Cash bonuses, salary increases, and other forms of compensation—yes, these are appreciated by employees. But far too many managers believe that the only thing employees want more of is money. Employees who are able to pay bills comfortably will look to other areas to keep them motivated to do their best work. Although compensation enables employees to do their jobs, it is your responsibility to find what enables employees to do their *best* jobs possible.

Money alone won't increase the level of performance of your employees. Positive reinforcement—praise and recognition, opportunities for growth and development, and so forth—is often what makes all the difference between an unmotivated and a motivated employee. In fact, as positive reinforcement brings improved employee performance, your company will see improved sales and revenues, which ultimately make it possible for increased employee payouts.

Essentially, nonmonetary incentives will be the key to improving employee productivity and higher financial gains for all. Monetary incentives, although tempting to implement, are often mere rewards of convenience; do little to establish links between behavior, incentives, and company values; and can even damage interpersonal relationships in the workplace. We'll dig deeper into the most effective nonmonetary incentives later in this chapter.

BUILDING A SYSTEM FOR REWARDING EMPLOYEES

Employees who are consistently motivated don't just suddenly arrive. You have to create a plan to reinforce and reward the behaviors you want them to enact:

Step 1: Establish an open and supportive environment in which your employees can thrive. Do this by figuring out what your workers value most.

Step 2: Create ways to thank, recognize, and acknowledge employees when they perform well. As different recognition opportunities arise, act on them.

Step 3: Work with employees on a continual basis to honestly address what they want and need.

Step 4: Follow your recognition plan as time goes on, but know that plans change and evolve, so be prepared!

Did you know employees are actually less motivated by fear of punishment and are more motivated by the possibility of earning rewards? In order to establish an effective and motivated workforce, you must thoroughly plan a rewards system and set in place. Here's how:

Establish understandable rules: Develop the specifics of your system of rewards by establishing clear parameters. Make sure targets are attainable and that all levels of employees have a chance to be recognized for their hard work.

Further organizational goals: Rewards that are effective should encourage job performances that contribute to the achievement of your organization's goals. A reward should decrease how often undesired behavior occurs and increase how often desired behavior occurs.

Acquire support and commitment: Both employees and managers should pledge direct involvement with your rewards program, and you should market your program on an ongoing basis.

Pay attention to what works: Is the rewards system you're implementing leading to your desired results? Link rewards closely with the behaviors you are looking to reinforce and be sure to change the rewards every so often in order to keep the system fresh.

HOW AND WHEN TO RECOGNIZE EMPLOYEES

The employees of the modern workplace not only want but also *expect* to be recognized for their good work. Despite this overwhelming need for recognition, a Globoforce WorkHuman Research Institute study revealed that 45 percent of US workers surveyed reported they had not been recognized on the job for at least six months, and 16 percent of US workers reported they had *never* been recognized on the job.[1]

Proper employee recognition generally asks that you consider the following:

Formality: Rewards can be given spontaneously and in more casual ways, like with a personal word of thanks or recognition during a meeting. An example of a more formal reward would be one given during a planned program, like an employee-of-the-month award.

Who provides the recognition: The significance of the recognition provider is something to consider. Does the employee most value the person who has an emotional significance to them, or do they most value the individual who has more professional status?

Type of recognition: Would the recipient of the recognition most value intangible recognition (public announcements, time off, ceremonies, etc.) or tangible recognition (a gift, trophy, or plaque)? When the recipient highly values the form recognition takes, that recognition becomes more meaningful and valuable to them.

Timing: In order to effectively shape desired behaviors, make sure positive reinforcement occurs frequently. This means recognition that reinforces performance must be frequent as well. At the same time, you must remember recognition should be given right after the desired behavior or performance. If recognition is not timely, it will not be meaningful!

Context and setting: When you give recognition, you may give it in public or in private. Take into account your employee's preference when making your decision.

Contingency: Contingency has to do with tying recognition closely to recognized behavior. Noncontingent recognition is generalized, whereas contingent recognition is specific, given to an employee after they exhibit a desired performance.

Be sure to regularly include recognition of employee success in private and public conversations and meetings. At the same time, unexpected celebrations are also effective. No matter the method, positive environments during times of organizational hardship can be created when the successes and strengths of employees are acknowledged.

Not only that, but employees are more likely to accomplish great results when managers focus on achievements, rather than emphasizing faults and negative results. Psychological research shows how positive reinforcement works better than negative reinforcement, because positive reinforcement increases the frequency of the desired behavior and creates good feelings among employees.

All in all, sometimes it just boils down to saying thank you—something not every employee gets to hear. Over half of employees report how the greatest motivating incentives are expressions of gratitude from managers. So, give thanks! And reward your employees for their big *and* small victories. You can praise your workers' achieving their goals, but you should be praising their progress toward them, too.

PEER-INITIATED RECOGNITION

Your employees will appreciate you recognizing their exem-
plary job performance, but peer recognition holds a most
unique importance to your workers. Peer recognition, seldom
expected, is often considered especially sincere and well-
earned. This is because employees had to assess and select one
of their own for praise and recognition.

Encourage employees to recognize other employees, and
initiate workplace programs or awards so peer-initiated recognition is more likely to occur. For instance, allow your employees to recognize model employees by having them vote on a
"People's Choice Award." Something like this inspires them to
notice the work of others more and develops camaraderie.

THE COMPLIMENT SANDWICH

The way you deliver a correction to an employee can have a
huge impact on whether it's received in the right way. Do it
wrong, and chances are the employee you're hoping to motivate may end up being demotivated by the experience. Consider this example of an employee whose behavior you want
to praise, but at the same time, correct:

> Hey, Susan—I just wanted to thank you for
> keeping the tables so clean for our customers.
> The problem is that some of the wait staff is
> complaining that you're playing favorites—
> certain people's tables get cleared right away,
> while others sit for fifteen or twenty minutes
> before you get to them. What's the problem?

The problem with this approach is that when you closely
follow a compliment with a correction, the employee isn't
going to hear the compliment—she's going to hear just the
correction. Although you do want the employee to correct
her behavior, you've spoiled your opportunity to praise the

employee and increase her motivation and engagement by putting the focus on the correction.

So, what's the solution? The compliment sandwich.

Bill Tobin owns and runs Tiki's Grill & Bar, the busiest independent restaurant in Waikiki. The restaurant has more than 180 staff on payroll, and its annual sales have grown in the double digits for the last five years running. Bill uses an approach to motivate his employees that he calls "the compliment sandwich." A *compliment sandwich* is when you place the correction "inside" of two compliments—just like you'd put a hamburger patty between the two halves of a bun.

As you're probably well aware, especially if you're a new manager or a new leader, some people have trouble finding the right words to say and are also nervous about directing people. Maybe they're not natural in the way they speak with people, or they're not comfortable giving feedback. The compliment sandwich is a great way for you to give employee recognition and corrections *and* teach the people who work for you to give feedback to others.

The idea behind the compliment sandwich is this: when you are giving feedback to an employee, first compliment them or say something positive. Then you give them something negative—the correction. That's the middle part of the sandwich—the patty in the bun. Then finish with something positive. You can reuse the positive you commented on earlier, but often managers using this method use two different positives on each side of the negative.

Here's an example: Let's say I'm a new manager who's training a busser. I say to the busser,

> "I want you to go clear and set this table."

The busser does it and comes back. I say,

> "Okay, that was a great job."

That's the first compliment.

> "But it took a bit more time than it should—
> we need to have these tables cleared in thirty
> seconds, not a minute, so we need to work on
> that a bit."

That's the correction.

> "But I really like your attention to detail.
> Great job!"

That's the second compliment.

When you follow this order in giving feedback—positive, negative, positive—you lessen the impact of the negative on an individual and you make the process easier on yourself by sticking with a proven process that's easy to remember. And for the leaders among you who may be a bit shy, the fact that you get to emphasize the positive makes it a more positive experience for *you,* too.

One thing to keep in mind about the compliment sandwich—Bill Tobin doesn't recommend using it if you're a senior leader working with senior people, if you're part of a team that has been together for long periods of time, or if you're a very experienced leader. If you're such a leader, you really need to learn to lead your people through frank and transparent communication, so when it's time for critical feedback, you can give it directly and to the point without needing to soften it up on either side with the sandwich.

DIGGING DEEPER INTO NONMONETARY INCENTIVES

"You get what you reward" is the most proven principle of performance management that's known to exist. In these fast-changing times, we need committed and engaged employees on the job. No company can afford to continue to employ men and women who aren't carrying their weight. And no company can afford not to make recognition and praise a key part of the way it does business. As we discussed earlier, the good news is that a powerful recognition program doesn't have to be expensive—in fact, it doesn't need to cost anything at all.

Ask employees what most motivates them to do a good job, and you'll find that money is almost never #1. In most surveys, money is not even in the top-five items named by employees. This fact has been confirmed in numerous studies.

Way back in 1946, the Labor Relations Institute of New York published the results of a survey of employees and managers, asking what factors were most important to employee job satisfaction.[2] When managers were asked what workplace factors were most important to their employees, they reported the following top-five things (out of a list of ten different items):

1. Good wages

2. Job security

3. Promotion/growth opportunities

4. Good working conditions

5. Interesting work

However, when the *workers* were asked the same question, a completely different set of answers emerged:

1. Full appreciation for work done

2. Feeling "in" on things

3. Sympathetic help on personal problems

4. Job security

5. Good wages[3]

In the decades since this survey, nothing much has changed when it comes to managers and their erroneous beliefs when it comes to employees. Managers are often convinced they know exactly what their employees want, but not only do they not really know, they wrongly assume that employees are primarily interested in such things as cash, job security, and promotions. As it turns out, nothing is farther from the truth. And, to the extent that some employees have focused on such things, it's managers and their self-fulfilling prophecies that have often made it so.

So, what's missing? How could managers get it so wrong? What do employees really want?

What employees really want is to be appreciated by their managers and by their companies for the good work they do—nothing more and nothing less. Let's now take a close look at some particularly effective ways to recognize employees for little or no money.

Low-end rewards. Low-end rewards are the kinds of thing that cost very little money and are easy to give out to employees. A classic example of a low-end reward is the gift card, which can be used for Starbucks, Amazon, Target, gas stations, and more.

Symbolic items. These could include anything from poker chips imprinted with a company logo that can be redeemed for gift cards at the end of the month, to caps, jackets, pens, coffee mugs, notebooks, and other inexpensive imprinted items that employees will be happy to receive and proud to use. The result of such programs is that employees are more focused on desired behaviors that are rewarded and they often have fun in the process of achieving their rewards.

Employer perks. These are nominal-cost items that a company or individual manager makes available to employees as a simple and thoughtful convenience. These can include such things as inexpensive breakfast or lunch items, water and sodas, snacks, and more.

Time-off rewards. Time itself can be effectively used as a form of recognition and reward. For example, you could give employees vouchers for time off, allow employees a bonus day off or a chance to "call in well," or you could make schedule adjustments or offer more scheduling flexibility. You could, for example, give deserving employees a free "I Don't Want to Get Out of Bed" day that they can redeem in the forthcoming year. Employees will love the benefit and consideration provided by the company—and their boss.

Constant attention. Ultimately, it's things a manager can do on a day-to-day basis that often have the most impact on any given employee's motivation: they can check in to ask how their employees are doing, ask them for their opinions, and thank them when they have done a good job or have gone above and beyond.

Here are some suggestions that managers can consider to show appreciation for their employees:

- For groups of employees, they can offer celebrations, team-building activities, morale-building meetings, team awards, and competitions.

- For individuals, they can implement one-on-one meetings, recognition activities, thanks, and praise.

THE POWER OF PRAISE

If you've got a pet dog, you already know the power of praise. (I leave out cats here since they seem to always have a mind of their own, at least until you start shaking their food bag.) When you praise your dog for fetching a ball or a stick that you've thrown, you're increasing the likelihood that he will perform again in exactly the same way.

This is also true of people. When you praise employees for doing something you want them to do on the job, you increase the likelihood that they will repeat the same behavior.

Praise can be delivered in three different ways: directly (in person, e.g., in the form of a simple spoken "thank you"), in front of others (publicly, e.g., in an eloquently written proclamation read by the CEO at an annual awards ceremony), and even when the employee being praised is not around (also known as *positive gossip*). Each one of these praise techniques is effective, although for entirely different reasons.

When you praise someone directly for their performance, you are making a very personal statement to the person: "I like what you did, and I'm proud of you for doing it." When you give someone praise directly, you have a number of approaches to choose from:

- Verbally (in person, or by phone call)

- In writing (by way of a note, letter, or memo)

- Electronically (by way of email message, text message, or website posting)

When you give an employee praise publicly, you amplify the power of the action many fold. This is because the person who receives the praise gets the opportunity to experience the pride of being called out in front of their peers for doing something right. Unfortunately, all too many employees don't get the attention of their manager unless they do something wrong. This makes being caught doing something right—especially in front of others—that much more powerful. Here are some common ways to publicly praise an employee:

- In a staff meeting

- In the hallway, while the employee is talking with coworkers

- In an email to the employee's team

- On a company or department bulletin board

- In an annual awards ceremony

Praising employees when they aren't around is a great way to spread your message of praise throughout an organization; eventually your good word will reach your intended target. But instead of being upset about this bit of gossip being told behind their backs, they'll be delighted. Much as giving praise publicly multiplies its effect, so too does praising someone when they aren't around. This is because the praise passes through the hands of a potentially large number of coworkers before it gets to the employee being praised—making it that much more valuable to the recipient. You can give praise when an employee isn't around in the following ways:

- Send an email to the employee's coworker praising something the employee did.

- Praise the employee at a staff meeting that they do not attend.

- Ask another manager to thank your employee for something that the employee did that you want to recognize.

Remember: praising an employee for a job well done costs you and your organization nothing, and there is no cap on the amount of praise you can give to your employees. Praise is the original renewable resource. Why not spread it around?

ACTION AGENDA

The key factors that most managers use to motivate employees today tend to be intangible, interpersonal, and relatively easy to implement.

The good news about recognizing and praising employees is that you can start taking action immediately—there's no need to wait and no need to create a budget or seek approval from corporate. Simply pick up the phone, or type up a quick email, or walk over to an employee and say, "Thank you!"

In the days and weeks that follow, I suggest you complete the following action agenda items:

1. Find out what things motivate your employees (by way of individual and group discussions, surveys, etc.).

2. Set specific group and individual goals.

3. Align appropriate recognition for goals achieved.

4. Repeat as necessary.

PART III

COMMON NEW BOSS CHALLENGES

To add value to others,
one must first value others.

—JOHN MAXWELL, author and speaker

Just as the global business environment is in a state of constant change and flux, so too are organizations and the people who work within them. This is resulting in a steady stream of challenges for the managers who are expected to solve problems and capitalize on opportunities. In this part, I focus on the most pressing of these challenges:

- Recruiting and retaining the best employees
- Dealing with employee problems
- Working through discipline and termination
- Tearing down organizational roadblocks
- Encouraging employees to experiment and take risks
- Managing a diverse workforce
- Handling office politics

11

Finders Keepers: Recruiting and Retaining the Best Employees

People are not your most important asset.
The right people are.

—JIM COLLINS, author

As a manager, one of the most significant responsibilities you have is to hire those who are the right fit for your organization. A great company is comprised of great hires, so don't underestimate the importance of the hiring process—it largely directs how successful your business will be as time goes by.

Not sure what qualities to look for in potential candidates? Consider these most important characteristics:

Takes initiative: Employees who take initiative at work are the very same employees who get ahead. If you recognize a candidate's ability to self-start, then you know you may have a potential hire on your hands.

Great attitude: You will be spending a lot of time with hires at the office, in meetings, or elsewhere. Will this candidate be enjoyable to be around? Remember, a positive attitude helps the job get done during successful *and* challenging times.

Has experience: Use the interview as an opportunity to confirm that the candidate can actually do the job. Experience in many positions is often necessary!

Works hard: Even if a candidate lacks training or experience, if they are hard-working, you know that they are more likely to execute tasks. Success is not guaranteed by skillset alone—a strong work ethic plays a powerful part here too. Just make sure work output is aligned with your company's goals and strategies.

Works well in a team: Today's organizations are largely comprised of teams. Is the candidate comfortable working with others? Do they understand the value of collaboration in the workplace?

Is resourceful: A smart hire is good, but a resourceful hire is great. Someone who is resourceful is not limited by their own intelligence—instead, they know how to navigate obstacles and find the resources available in order to find the best solutions at a more rapid pace.

Fits into company culture: Businesses and organizations have different missions and values. Your company culture is entirely unique, and even if a candidate looks good on paper, it does not mean they will necessarily gel with your company.

Is dedicated: Not only do you want a qualified candidate, but you also want a dedicated and loyal candidate. Hiring and training are costly endeavors for any company—that's why you want a hire who will stay at your position for years. Learn more about the candidate's job stability by inquiring about length of employment at their previous employers.

HOW TO RECRUIT THE VERY BEST

The quality of your business is a direct reflection of the quality of the people you hire. Great hires color and invigorate the office experience, and bad hires frustrate staff, waste time, and cost your business money. In order to select the best applicants for the job, you need to create a pool of applicants to select from. The good news is that great applicants can be found everywhere.

Utilizing Traditional Recruitment Channels

When you're recruiting new employees, here are some methods to successfully find the exact candidates you need:

Use an employment agency: Need to fill a highly specialized position? Less interested in doing recruitment and applicant screening yourself? Employment agencies can find the qualified candidates you are in search of, but be aware that they are often pricey.

Consider professional associations: Depending on your profession, you may have an already prescreened audience who can help you find candidates. This audience is an association that looks out for you—for example, doctors often belong to the American Medical Association.

Utilize temporary agencies: Sometimes, important positions need to be filled immediately. Hiring temporary employees will get necessary work done and buy you more time to find the perfect candidate. You may even find that the temporary employee is talented enough to be hired into a full-time position.

Look internally: Perhaps your next hire is already a part of your organization! Look outside your company only after assessing internal options. If you recruit from within, you will save money and have a much easier hiring process. You can also look to personal referrals from employees and coworkers.

Taking Advantage of the Internet

Physical job advertisements do still exist, but the Internet has, for the most part, taken their place. Recruitment can now be entirely digital, so make sure you take advantage of the internet's power as you search for new hires.

Create a website: When you establish an online presence for your business, you make it clear that your company will stay relevant in today's digital age. Plus, if you set up a blog for your company, staff can go into detail about their jobs and the company culture—descriptions like these can entice potential candidates.

Create an email campaign: Have a company newsletter with tons of subscribers? Send an email blast with information on job openings to spread the word about current recruitment.

Use social networking: Social platforms like Facebook and Twitter can give you immediate, real-time access to prospective job applicants. You can also disperse information about open positions to tons of users and potential candidates at the click of a button, through posts and tweets. Consider also using LinkedIn, which was actually created for employers to connect with job seekers. You can reach candidates on LinkedIn either by utilizing paid job advertisements on the platform or by way of your LinkedIn company page or employee profiles. These social media platforms are free to use (except in the case of paid job ads), can be very effective, and coexist with more conventional (and still usable) job-hunting websites like Monster.com or CareerBuilder.com.

MASTERING THE INTERVIEW

Do you know your interviewing style? Are you the interviewer who prepares for the interview moments before it actually takes place, or do you spend hours (or days) reviewing the job description, writing questions, and pouring over resumes? It's no secret that becoming a great interviewer requires thorough preparation. Here's how to properly master the interviewing process.

Questions You Should Ask

You want your interviewee to give you the best answers they can, answers that clearly signal to you if the candidate is a good fit for your company. But if you want great answers, you must ask great questions. Interview questions generally fall into one of four categories:

How can you uniquely contribute to this organization? You may be interviewing a slew of highly qualified candidates who have impressive work ethics, incredible personalities, and rich experiences. But the key to learning who should be your next hire lies in the answer to the question, "What can you do for this business?" Focus less on what your firm can give to the candidate and more on what your candidate can give to the firm.

What brings you here? Why is a candidate taking the time to sit with you today? Is it because of a mere need of employment or income, or does this candidate know that your firm is where they belong?

How do you describe yourself? Because you will be spending many of your working hours with employees, make sure you are spending time with hires you like being around. This question also allows you to get a sense of the kind of workers they are, because their answers will reveal if they consider themselves to be hard-working, trustworthy, honest, and/or ethical.

Is our pay range acceptable? Top candidates may be highly qualified, but perfect candidates are highly qualified *and* affordable.

The Do's of Interviewing

Give a fantastic interview to get a fantastic hire. Follow these interviewing do's:

Review resumes before the interview: It's best to review each interviewee's resume the morning of interviews, not at the time of the interview itself. Early review allows you to address details that pique your interest.

Know the job description: Don't surprise your potential hires with new duties and requirements during the interview. Instead, communicate job responsibilities clearly in advance in the job listing.

Write up questions beforehand: What skills and experience are you looking for in candidates? Make a checklist, and craft questions that will give you valuable insight into the applicant.

Take notes: We all like to think we have superior memories, but the reality is we sometimes forget important details said by candidates. Write down responses and even your first impressions of interviewees.

The Don'ts of Interviewing

You know now what you *should* do during the interview process, but what kinds of actions should you absolutely avoid? Some don'ts have much to do with maintaining professionalism and following appropriate business practices. For instance, it's best to decline any date invitations you receive from applicants.

Even further, some mistakes you make during the interview process could land you in hot water. Discrimination can occur during interviews if you ask the wrong questions. For example, in the US, you are not allowed to ask if an applicant is disabled; however, you are able to ask if a candidate can successfully fulfill certain tasks. Depending on the situation, asking about the following subjects can result in legal trouble: age, disability, race, religion, sexual orientation, sex, criminal record, height and weight, national origin. No matter what, center your questions around the abilities of the candidate and the criteria relevant to the job.

STACKING UP YOUR CANDIDATES

After narrowing down the applicant pool to a few high-quality people, you get to make a definitive decision on who to hire. But not without first doing some additional research on your candidates.

Checking References

If a resume seems too good to be true, checking references is an effective way to confirm someone is who they say they are. Even if an applicant seems trustworthy, avoid hiring new staff members without conducting a thorough background check.

Reference checking also gives you deeper insight into how prospective employees work and what they're like in social situations. Consider checking academic references and contact previous supervisors to learn about past work experience. And, as always, the Internet is at your beck and call. Utilize search engines or look at social media profiles to uncover more details about a potential hire.

Hiring the Best

As you spend time ranking candidates, you want to keep a few tips in mind in order to make the best hiring decision possible. For example, practice objectivity during this process, and focus on facts and qualifications, not style or charming personalities. What qualities indicate a candidate's ability to perform, and what qualities should not influence your choice? Eliminate bias in your thinking and remember that diversity helps grow organizations.

If you are having difficulty choosing between multiple incredibly skilled and qualified candidates (even after reviewing objective data), trust your gut. Allow some subjectivity in the decision-making process; consider also giving candidates tasks and comparing their results.

Lastly, sometimes there is no clear-cut winning candidate during a round of hiring. It is perfectly acceptable to revisit the candidate pool, and to see who, with a little bit of training, could really unleash their potential and contribute to your company. If no one stands out to you, don't fill a position just to fill it. Wait for the right fit for your organization, or you will face the damages created by an inadequate hire.

12

Uh-Oh—Dealing with Employee Problems

Don't be embarrassed by your failures.
Learn from them and start again.

—RICHARD BRANSON, founder of Virgin Group

To many of us, the word *discipline* doesn't exactly bring about happy memories whether on the job or in our personal lives. But what does *discipline* mean to you? Does your organization define it differently, or has it always had a negative connotation? Has there ever been a moment in which employees (or you) looked forward to being disciplined?

The truth is, the terms *discipline* and *punishment* mean the same thing in the eyes of employees. But the reality is much different. Employee discipline can actually be a positive experience when done the correct way. The disciplinary process can provide guidance and training for employees so they can perform better. Discipline can also bring certain issues or concerns to light so employees may take correctional action.

Depending on the work history of the involved employee and the nature of the problem as well as its severity, there is a wide range of available methods for discipline. An employee may be terminated, or they may be given verbal counsel ("Your budget was turned in three days after the deadline. I expect all budgets to be submitted on time."). If the problem is frequently repeated and the employee does not have a clean performance record, you may adjust your method of disciplinary action as you see fit.

Employees are generally disciplined for these two main reasons:

Misconduct: If an employee behaves inappropriately or in ways unacceptable to you, the organization, or the law, they can find themselves facing disciplinary action.

Performance problems: Each position has an array of goals that need to be met, as part of the job. When an employee fails to meet these goals, some sort of discipline should be administered.

A manager practices effective discipline by paying attention to when an employee's performance falls short or when an employee misbehaves. In fact, the best managers take note of these instances long before these problems become major areas of concern and get out of hand. Effective managers know to guide their employees along the right paths and also understands that if they do not discipline their employees at the right time, they as managers are ultimately at fault if poor performance continues or misconduct escalates.

Don't forget: the goal of discipline isn't to punish employees. It's to help them better perform their jobs.

When is the right time for discipline? It is highly recommended that you do not put it off. It should be carried out as soon as any problem occurs. If you allow too much time between an incident that occurs and discipline, not only will employees forget incident specifics, but they will also believe the problem is not serious since it was not addressed immediately.

If you decide to postpone discipline (whether temporarily or indefinitely), you are doing a massive disservice to all those employees who perform well for your organization. Ultimately, you must remember that you get what you condone or reward. If you are inadvertently reinforcing negative behavior and poor performance by rewarding it or simply allowing it, you may find yourself disciplining employees more frequently than you would like.

FOCUSING ON PERFORMANCE, NOT PERSONALITIES

As a manager, it is not your job to figure out why employees act the way they do or to deconstruct and understand an employee's personality. You were hired to manage, not to be the acting psychologist. Your responsibility is to assess employee performance, especially against agreed-upon standards and expectations. To put it simply, when employees are performing well, you motivate and reward them; when employees perform below standard, you learn what is causing this unsatisfactory performance and make corrections or discipline if necessary.

This, however, does not mean you should rule out compassion while you're on the job. Life can throw any of us tremendous challenges that lead to hard times. When your employees experience these—whether they come in the form of family challenges or financial problems—you should do what you can to help them get through their difficulties. However, they will always have to eventually meet performance standards, because allowing different performance standards for different employees will invariably lead to a dysfunctional organization with unhappy people.

Discipline that you apply should be administered in a consistent and fair fashion. This means that before you discipline an employee, you have focused on performance levels, and you haven't jumped to conclusions or judgment before you have acquired all the facts behind an employee's situation or inability to perform well. Act without favoritism, communicate performance standards clearly to all hires, and make sure all employees fully understand company policy. You may guide your employees, but remember, in the end, how they perform and behave is in their hands.

REASONS SOME MANAGERS AVOID DEALING WITH EMPLOYEE ISSUES

Few managers prefer to spend their mornings disciplining employees or dealing with employee issues. Even if you have clear and obvious reasons for counseling, disciplining, or even firing an employee, the task isn't a particularly pleasant one. But the sooner you address employee performance problems, the sooner they will be resolved. Don't let the following reasons affect the time it takes for you to deal with employee performance issues:

Emotional involvement: You may become friends with some of your employees since you will be spending a lot of time with them. However, this can become a problem if you have developed an emotional attachment to someone you will need to discipline or fire.

How it makes you look: If an employee has to be disciplined or fired, does that mean that you have failed as a manager? Don't put up with poor performance in the workplace just because you are concerned these performance problems will actually shed light on your own shortcomings.

Fear of legal action: If the possibility of legal action makes you uneasy, then you might be tempted to postpone employee discipline or termination. This will only lead to growing and festering problems. Meet with a lawyer or your company's general counsel to explore your legal options.

Fear of the unknown: How employees react when they are disciplined or fired is not something you can predict. There may be an emotional outburst you are not equipped to handle, for example. In order to get past this fear, study the firing process, check in with human resources to get support, or sit in on another employee's discipline and termination before you conduct one yourself.

CREATING AN IMPROVEMENT PLAN

In need of a plan for employee discipline? The *performance improvement plan,* an important part of the discipline process, outlines what steps an employee needs to take within a certain timeframe in order to improve their performance.

Minor performance transgressions won't need such a plan because verbal counseling should be enough. In addition, employee misconduct cannot be corrected by the performance improvement plan either, since misconduct should be corrected immediately. But if the employee in question is making habitual mistakes that require more severe disciplinary measures, it's a different story. In that instance, a performance plan is just what you need. It's comprised of three parts:

Goal statement: What does satisfactory improvement look like? Tied to performance standards, this goal could be, for example, "Submit all weekly reports on or before confirmed deadlines."

A schedule: A plan cannot be successful without a schedule. Include a definite completion date, and even fixed dates for plan milestones. This portion could say something like: "Attain this goal within four months of creation of this plan."

Required training and resources: This involves a summary of training and resources that will bring an employee's performance to acceptable standards: "Enroll in a three-week program on time management."

IMPLEMENTING THE PLAN

Once a plan is created, it is crucial that it is actually followed. When you set up performance improvement plans with employees, you must also pay careful attention to their progress. Follow up with your employees to make sure the plan is being acted on rather than abandoned. Check in on the advancements they have made, if they are keeping to the schedule, and if you are adequately providing the training and resources they said they would be utilizing.

Schedule progress report meetings on a consistent basis; these will not only give you important information about their progress, but these meetings will also prove to your employees that you are invested in their improvements. If an employee cannot maintain performance up to standards, you may have to consider how suitable they are for employment at your organization.

13

When Good People Go Bad: Discipline and Termination

If we don't discipline ourselves,
the world will do it for us.

—WILLIAM FEATHER, publisher and author

As you might recall from the previous chapter, when it comes time to discipline an employee, it will most often be for either problems of performance or misconduct. Performance problems are usually fixed with correct training and guidance and are not entirely an employee's fault. Issues with performance are also often less severe transgressions that require less severe disciplinary action than those associated with misconduct—this is because misconduct is typically an act an employee carries out willfully.

A two-track disciplinary system that addresses either performance or misconduct reflects something called *progressive discipline.* In order to attain the behavior you want using progressive disciplinary action, you need to exercise the least severe disciplinary step. For example, if an employee does not improve their performance after you give them a verbal warning, you may proceed to a written warning. Your goal with progressive discipline is to help your employee understand which behavior to correct before you have to exercise severe actions like demotions, pay reductions, or firing.

Before you move forward with discipline, discern if performance or misconduct needs to be corrected. Then decide the severity of the transgression and how to best communicate your response to the employee's actions.

HANDLING PERFORMANCE ISSUES

Even though different companies assess performance in different ways, employees generally have either unacceptable, acceptable, or outstanding performance. Discipline is utilized in cases of unacceptable performance, when employees fail to meet standards and need to correct the areas in which they fall short.

Here is a list of disciplinary steps ordered from least to most severe. To successfully discipline an employee, apply progressive discipline principles and begin with the least severe step when you are trying to get the behavior you want. Should this step not change your employee's behavior for the better, apply the step that follows.

Step 1: Verbal counseling: The most common disciplinary form, this is usually a step that managers take first in order to correct behavior or performance. It can be formal, taking place in a meeting, or it can be given casually, in passing.

Step 2: Written counseling: If verbal counseling is not effective, written counseling is utilized, which documents the employee's performance. Generally, written counseling leads to verbal discussions about plans for improvement.

Step 3: Negative performance evaluation: If verbal and written counseling don't yield results, consider this option, which can be exercised at any time.

Step 4: Demotion: Although a demoralizing move, this step will improve performance because it shifts employees into jobs and positions they can handle or excel at.

Step 5: Termination: Firing an employee is often a last resort after all other options have failed. Remember to document employee shortcomings and performance well to prevent a lawsuit for wrongful termination.

HANDLING MISCONDUCT

Misconduct is in its own lane, with its own track of discipline. It cannot be handled the same way performance problems are handled. As a more major transgression, misconduct reveals existing shortcomings of employee attitudes, beliefs, or ethics. Notice the difference in language when it comes to disciplinary steps for misconduct (i.e., verbal *counseling* becomes verbal *warnings*).

As a manager, you must handle misconduct in more serious ways than you do performance issues. Improved employee performance takes time to achieve, but misconduct must cease immediately, especially if the offense committed has major legal implications for you or your business. The following discipline steps increase in severity, and what you choose to exercise will align with your employee's record and how serious their offense is.

Step 1: Verbal warning: Handle first offenses and minor acts of misconduct with verbal warnings, with which you tell employees that their behavior is unacceptable and must not continue any further.

Step 2: Written warning: If verbal warnings are ignored or not understood, or if the offense requires a more serious disciplinary action, use a written warning to let your employees know the severity of the situation at hand.

Step 3: Reprimand: Serious misconduct, or misconduct that is repeated, necessitates a reprimand, which typically looks like a written warning. A manager higher up gives reprimands.

Step 4: Suspension: This mandatory leave is without pay, and an employee is removed from the office in order to preserve employee morale or safety. A non-disciplinary suspension can also occur if misconduct charges are being investigated (the employee is typically paid during this time of case review).

Step 5: Termination: Aside from repeated misconduct, some serious incidents (theft, safety violations, and other serious misconduct) warrant firing employees.

HOW TO DISCIPLINE AN EMPLOYEE

Regardless of the disciplinary actions you choose, how you handle the situation at hand matters. Ultimately you want employees to understand what is wrong, how they contribute to the issue, and how to rectify things. You can accomplish this by creating a discipline script. Here's how to do so, ensuring that you discipline employees the right way.

Step 1: Detail incorrect behavior: Be incredibly detailed when you describe what your employee is doing wrong. What, exactly, is unacceptable? When did it occur? Remember to emphasize employee behavior and focus less on the employee. It's not personal, it's business.

Step 2: Describe how work is affected: Staff must know how unacceptable behavior affects not only other employees, but also the work being produced.

Step 3: Express what needs to change: You can tell someone what they have done wrong, but what is most crucial is that you tell them how to make things right.

Step 4: Discuss consequences: Naturally, should poor performance continue, have a conversation with your employee and outline the consequences that are a result of their actions.

Step 5: Give support: If you want employees to improve, you must lend them genuine support. Even asking how you can assist them will work wonders.

One complete statement drawn from the steps in this discipline script, although simple, often leads to seriously positive changes in the workplace. An example script is as follows:

> You have not been punctual every day of this week. Because of your inability to arrive on time, you have missed critical details from meetings, and projects have not been completed. If you are late one more time, you will be given a reprimand by my higher-up. But let's work to avoid this action. I know you're capable of being on time!

NOT EVERY TERMINATION IS CREATED EQUAL

There are a number of reasons to terminate employment and the types of termination are divided into two categories: voluntary and involuntary. For instance, with *voluntary terminations,* sometimes employees are offered better pay somewhere else, or they leave for personal reasons or other issues. Here are other, common examples of voluntary terminations:

Voluntary resignation: If employees quit their positions on their own accord, you may actually learn some valuable information from such resignations. You cannot keep an employee at your company forever, but you can ensure that the employees you have do not willfully leave because of company inadequacies. Hold exit interviews with quitting employees to learn about existing company problems and potential solutions.

Encouraged resignation: One way to help an employee save face before being fired is to encourage them to resign. This voluntary termination keeps an employee's record clean and relieves some of the pain of an actual firing.

Retirement: When employees complete their professional lives and choose to terminate employment forever, they are retiring. Unlike encouraged or unprompted resignation, retirement is generally celebrated!

INVOLUNTARY TERMINATIONS

Sometimes, however, termination is carried out against the employee's will entirely; this is an *involuntary termination*. Involuntary terminations, which are rarely enjoyable, usually arrive in one of two forms:

Firing: An employee is fired when there is no hope of correcting their performance, when the person employed does not successfully adapt or grow with their role in a changing business landscape, or when they are responsible for serious misconduct.

Layoffs: Due to financial reasons, a company may decide to let go of a specific number of employees. This is called a *layoff,* and it occurs, for example, if a company has to reduce payroll costs in order to stay in business. Check your company policy in order to learn the protocol for layoff order. Sometimes job performance determines who is laid off, and in other instances, seniority affects who is let go.

FIRING AN EMPLOYEE

No one enjoys firing an employee. Not only is the termination process generally unpleasant, but it's also lengthy and complicated. You probably have a lot of questions as a manager regarding the logistics of such a process too.

When, for example, is the best time to fire an employee? The answer is to start the termination process once you decide letting someone go is necessary. Don't waste more company time and resources by postponing the termination.

Perhaps you are wondering how to best protect yourself before firing someone. At a time when even a slight oversight can result in serious monetary damage for a company, it's critical that you do everything possible to avoid wrongful termination charges. Document employee performance and all proof that supports your claims. Check to see that you communicated clearly defined and reasonable performance standards, that you provided fair warning in response to unsatisfactory behavior and performance, and that you gave an appropriate amount of time for an employee to improve behavior.

As you begin the termination procedure, involve your department of human resources—this allows for a smooth and legal process. Give clear reasons behind the firing, and preserve employee dignity (this, in turn, will then curtail growing resentment against you and your organization) by holding the termination meeting in a private space, by being calm and professional, and by showing understanding and empathy. Even though there is much prep-work to be done before termination occurs, the steps for firing someone are few in number and are quite simple:

Step 1: State that you have made the decision to terminate their employment.

Step 2: Cite policies and give a thorough explanation behind the termination.

Step 3: Communicate the effective date of termination and inform them of other relevant details regarding their exit.

LAYING OFF AN EMPLOYEE

Different from firings is the layoff, which happens when your business has to go through painful downsizing and company restructuring. This is normally not a direct fault of the employees, who are often loyal, productive, and high-achieving workers. Instead, other factors are to blame, such as a rapidly changing market, increased competition in the marketplace, or acquisitions.

When you must conduct a layoff, first get your department of human resources (HR) involved. HR can assist in creating a smooth and law-abiding termination process. Next, freeze

hiring, and spread the news of planned layoffs as early as possible to your staff—they will need advanced notice of company changes. Then you can start compiling a list of who to
let go, keeping workers who are most skilled, experienced, and
critical for your organization's success.

Follow company procedure as you rank staff members for
layoff and begin holding private conversations regarding their
termination status. Go over the exit process in detail—discuss
benefits, severance packages, and other arrangements. Once
layoffs are completed, assemble your remaining staff members and move toward a more successful and stable company
future.

WHEN BAD BEHAVIOR WARRANTS IMMEDIATE TERMINATION

No one wants to fire an employee, but sometimes you may be
left with little choice. This is definitely the case when employee
behavior is so far out of bounds that keeping an employee
around puts your other employees, your customers, your community, and your business at risk. A number of offenses merit
immediate termination, even without giving discipline first
(reprimand, written warning, verbal counseling, or suspension). The following behaviors are examples:

Theft: When employees are caught engaging in theft, be
sure to obtain proof. Then you know you will be in good
legal standing if you decide to terminate an employee and
they decide to pursue legal action.

Sexual harassment: Intolerable offenses in this category involve requests for sexual favors, unwelcome sexual
advances, and other verbal or physical sexual conduct.

Incompetence: Sometimes, no matter how much effort
you put into training an employee, they simply are not
cut out for the job. If you have given your all when trying
to help an employee improve, and they still can't perform

at satisfactory levels of competence, letting this worker go may be in the best interest of both the employee and the organization.

Coming to work under the influence of drugs or alcohol: Being intoxicated on the job is sufficient grounds for immediate termination, but many companies also offer employees the chance to undergo counseling through approved programs.

Insubordination: Employees are hired to carry out decisions. Many supervisors allow employees to question the *why* behind a decision, but ultimately an employee has to be willing to follow your direction. If the employee deliberately refuses to complete the tasks they have been instructed to carry out, immediate termination can occur.

Always late: A successful company is comprised of workers who complete jobs on time. Repeated and unexcused tardiness sets a bad example for punctual employees, and most of all, it affects scheduled task completion.

Verbal abuse and physical violence: You and your employees have a right to perform your jobs in a safe environment, free of harassment, verbal abuse, and physical danger. Violence should be taken seriously. You can immediately fire employees who are physically or verbally abusive, and law enforcement can be called to assist in removing individuals who engage in this and other harmful behavior.

Fraudulent acts: No need to employ anyone who has falsified records! If you discover that an employee has provided fraudulent information during the hiring process (for example, fake experience or degrees) or while on the job (for example, falsified timecards or bogus expense reports), you may immediately dismiss them.

14

Tearing Down
Organizational Roadblocks

We think it's important for employees to have
fun ... it drives employee engagement.

—TONY HSIEH, CEO, Zappos

The vast majority of organizations—businesses small and large, nonprofits, and government—have a tremendous problem today. That problem is a lack of employee engagement. Polling organization Gallup keeps very close tabs on the state of employee engagement, which the organization defines as how involved in and enthusiastic employees are about their work and workplace.

In its most recent *State of the American Workplace* report, Gallup's chairman and CEO, Jim Clifton, had this to say about the situation:

The American workforce has more than 100 million full-time employees. One-third [33%] of those employees are what Gallup calls engaged at work. They love their jobs and make their organization and America better every day. At the other end, 16% of employees are actively disengaged—they

*are miserable in the workplace and destroy what the most
engaged employees build. The remaining 51% of employees
are not engaged—they're just there.[1]*

As you can see, these statistics are abysmal. What's worse
is that they haven't changed all that much over the years that
Gallup has been tracking them. In 2001, for example, 30 percent of employees surveyed by Gallup were engaged in their
work and workplace, 54 percent were not engaged, and 16 percent were actively disengaged.[2]

The good news is that, as a manager, you have the power
to change this. You have the tools—and the duty—to create a
workplace and culture that encourages and fosters employee
engagement.

Do you know the first step toward employee empowerment and initiative? If you think the answer has to do with
giving motivational speeches and words of inspiration, you
may be ignoring the incredible power of effective day-to-day
communication. When you honestly and openly communicate with your employees, you are taking the first step toward
fostering employee involvement, which can ultimately work
in your favor. This is because when employees are armed with
relevant information on a more frequent basis, they can make
decisions and move forward in ways that will be in your organization's best interests. Not only will your daily operations
improve, but you can also attain an improved bottom line.

Gallup's Jim Clifton suggests that by following these steps,
you can begin the transformation of an unengaged workforce
into one that is fully engaged:

Step 1: Call an executive committee meeting and commit
to transforming your workplace from old command-and-control to one of high development and ongoing coaching
conversations.

Step 2: Dive in—don't put your toe in. You can afford a lot
of mistakes and even failures because the system you currently use doesn't work anyway.

Step 3: Switch from a culture of "employee satisfaction"—which only measures things like how much workers like their perks and benefits—to a "coaching culture."

Step 4: Change from a culture of "paycheck" to a culture of "purpose."[3]

So, what does it take to become a manager who effectively communicates with and involves workers? We will explore ways you can become a manager who is more engaged with employees in the following sections.

WHY ENGAGEMENT?

The state of employee engagement is something every manager should be concerned about. Why? Because it has a direct and compelling impact on employee performance, and ultimately, the performance of the organization. Aon Hewitt and the Queen's Center for Business Venturing (QCBV) teamed up to determine the relationship between employee engagement and employee performance. According to their research, organizations with the most engaged employees achieve

- 65 percent greater share-price increase
- 26 percent less employee turnover
- 100 percent more unsolicited employment applications
- 20 percent less absenteeism
- 15 percent greater employee productivity
- Up to 30 percent greater customer satisfaction levels[4]

An organization's culture and people practices have an impact on the effectiveness of its employees, which in turn has a direct impact on the business. The four critical employee attitude factors that drive financial performance are commitment, line of sight, enablement, and integrity.

Organizations with high employee *commitment* create more than six times the surplus value (economic value in excess of assets) than those with low commitment. How can you tell whether employees are committed? Many factors contribute to this; however, if you want a quick acid test, consider these leading indicators:

- Employees are proud to work for your company, perceive it as better than others, and recommend it as a good place to work.

- Employee satisfaction is high and people stay with your company even when similar positions are available elsewhere.

The second factor, *line of sight,* exists when employees know what to do to make their organization successful. Organizations with high line of sight create more than double the surplus value created by organizations with low line of sight. Employees feel a strong line of sight when

- They understand the company's business goals, the steps that will be taken to achieve them, and the way their own individual contributions fit into the picture.

- They receive information that measures how well their organization is doing compared to its goals.

An effective performance management system is critical for driving line of sight; unfortunately, *effective* and *performance management* are often separate concepts. People need to understand their goals and believe they are doable, know how to do them, and feel they are rewarded for their efforts.

Like line-of-sight, *enablement* can double the surplus economic value of an organization. Enablement is measured by determining whether we are providing employees with the training, resources, tools, and equipment they need to do their jobs. To some extent, enablement reflects the empowerment of the individual. We can tell whether it exists by looking at things such as whether employees

- Receive the training they need to be effective
- Have the resources they need to be effective

- Have reasonable workloads
- Have a say in how their work is done
- Have enough colleagues to get the work done

Employee involvement in decisions is a very critical factor in the enablement area—management really must consider employees and involve them in decisions that affect them.

The final key factor is *integrity*. Integrity exists when employees understand and live up to their company's values and expect others (particularly leaders) to do the same. Again, the impact of integrity is significant. Companies with low integrity scores generated roughly half the surplus economic value as those with high scores. We look at these indicators to determine whether employees believe there is integrity in the workplace:

- They have confidence in senior management.
- They believe that senior managers respond to unethical behavior.
- They believe that the employer acts with honesty and integrity.
- They believe the information they receive from management.

The importance of employee engagement and an effective work environment has been confirmed in many ways and by many organizations. For example, the Corporate Leadership Council (CLC) conducted major research on the attitudes of member companies' employees. In this study, the council looked at 300 different levers available to organizations to drive discretionary effort and improve performance. They found that 50 were noticeably more effective at creating discretionary effort among employees. These *engagement levers* were surprisingly consistent across all employee segments (managers, hourly workers, front-line employees, salespeople, Gen Xers and Yers, and so forth).[5]

The top ten levers are organizational rather than driven by individual managers. If we equate *commitment* to *engagement,* then these factors drive engagement of the workforce:

TOP TEN LEVERS OF ENGAGEMENT: CORPORATE LEADERSHIP COUNCIL

1. Connection between work and organizational strategy
2. Importance of job to organizational success
3. Understanding of how to complete work projects
4. Internal communication
5. Demonstrates strong commitment to diversity
6. Demonstrates honesty and integrity
7. Reputation of integrity
8. Adapts to changing circumstances
9. Clearly articulates organizational goals
10. Possesses job skills[6]

The CLC study also distinguishes between an employee's *rational commitment* (which is driven by factors such as competitive pay and basic working conditions) and their *emotional commitment.* Although having a rational commitment can make it less likely that an employee will leave and more likely that they'll contribute some effort, emotional commitment is what has the greatest impact on the discretionary effort of the individual.

Employees must have some rational commitment if they're going to stay, but they must also have emotional commitment to achieve outstanding success. The most effective organizations provide strong leadership, flexible work arrangements, protections for individuals, broad-based reward systems, and an approach to performance and justice that is blind to status.

How does your workplace stack up to all of this?

FOSTERING FOCUS

The managers and workers of today are entering a new and unique partnership within the modern workplace. Instead of only directing and giving orders to their employees, today's managers have to establish and nurture an office environment that encourages employees to contribute more. Namely, employees are encouraged to find ways to overcome company challenges, to pursue and discover new sources of opportunity for the company, and to share their best pieces of work and ideas. In order to properly guide employees to do this, managers should consider asking their workers the following questions:

- How can you improve and implement new ideas for new services or products?

- How can we improve employee teamwork and morale, especially in cost-efficient ways?

- Do you know how much you and your coworkers affect the bottom line of the company?

- What are the steps we as an organization need to take in order to save money, resources, and time?

ASKING FOR EMPLOYEE INPUT

Does your organization ever encourage employees to speak up about concerns, suggestions, or thoughts? Are your people willing to speak up about these kinds of things? When you begin to consistently solicit ideas from your staff, you aren't just increasing employee participation—you're also opening the door for some seriously beneficial results, like how to streamline processes, get better at customer service, and save or make money.

Make it a point to directly ask workers what they think about policies and practices—don't just rely on end-of-meeting surveys or unused suggestion boxes. Challenge employees to find new areas of improvement and let them know how important their input is to the success of the company. Each employee has the ability to come up with a game-changing idea. Your job as a manager is to bring this idea out into the world so it can be implemented.

LETTING EMPLOYEES GET INVOLVED IN DECISIONS

We know that most of the time, decisions regarding company changes come from high-level employees. But how do we know these are the best decisions we could make? Shouldn't decisions be influenced by the people who actually work in affected jobs or departments, not just from managers or executives?

Giving employees agency in decision-making is one powerful way to effectively attain employee participation and company-wide buy-in. This is often because when you ask your staff for their feedback, it demonstrates that you respect and trust them. In addition to asking employees for their opinions on important department matters, invite them to set goals for their departments.

Also, make sure successful ideas and solutions are properly recognized—rewards like cash incentives acknowledge an employee's hard work and foresight and inspire others to find additional improvements.

Ultimately, you don't want your staff to believe decisions are made without considering their input. If your employees think their input does not matter, then they will feel less inclined to share their thoughts and critiques with you. And, a lack of proper feedback will put a roadblock on your company's path to improvement and success.

If employees get to develop their own suitable work plans, work becomes purposeful, and employees become fully engaged. As you involve your employees more in the workplace, find ways to increase employee autonomy, whether it's by encouraging them to find new ideas and use new resources or by allowing them to take specific actions in order to complete their duties. The workers of today are most motivated by flexible work schedules, authority, and autonomy. When you provide these and other motivators, employee morale, engagement, and performance will improve.

THE POWER OF THE FLEXIBLE WORK SCHEDULES AND ARRANGEMENTS

Flexible work schedules offer a variety of benefits to employees and employers alike. Studies show that well-rounded employees have reduced stress, often because they are involved in activities outside of work and have better work-life balance. So, consider implementing four-day work weeks and allowing telecommuting or alternate work hours (for example, letting employees arrive late and leave late) if such arrangements don't interfere with serving customers or getting work done efficiently and effectively.

No matter what methods you decide to implement, work with your employees to make flexible schedules possible. Not only will they appreciate the decreased commuting time and increased time spent at home with family, but your company will also be rewarded with increased productivity.

With changing technological advances come changing business conduct and new ways for employees to work. As more and more companies utilize digital platforms, more and more tasks can be completed without workers needing to be present in a physical office. This is why a number of organizations have taken steps to implement flexible schedules and options for telecommunicating.

Remote work can be an idea some managers take time to warm up to, but you will reap the benefits when you treat your employees as if they are responsible. Doing so gives them a sense of empowerment and purpose. Still not convinced?

Consider the following statistics from a report published by job site Indeed:

- Fifty-two percent of employees wish they could work from home.

- Nearly half of employees—47 percent—say that whether or not a company has a remote work policy is important to them when they are looking for a job.

- More than one-third of employees—40 percent—would consider taking a pay cut to be able to work remotely.

- For those employees who work from home, 75 percent say that they have an improved work-life balance as a result, and 57 percent believe they are more productive when working from home.[7]

Creating a sense of personal and work-life balance largely has to do with employees' desires to retain their own identities. Even if many employees believe their jobs are part of who they are, they might not always want it to be this way. Encourage employees to delve more into their interests outside of the office—for them, this creates a good work-life balance, which is critical for productivity and overall health.

HOW TO SUPPORT EMPLOYEES AS A MANAGER

Take note: according to a study by Gallup, 51 percent of currently employed US adults are actively looking for a new job, or are watching for new job opportunities.[8] Why? In many cases, this is because employees don't feel that their managers support them or their decisions. This shows that managers have a long way to go when it comes to properly motivating and supporting employees.

Need some tips on ensuring that your employees feel supported? Here are a few:

Show that you understand: Meet employees with understanding and empathy. The more they feel that you are

rooting for them, the more stable they will be—your business will do well because of this.

Give support even when mistakes are made: Some managers criticize employees who mess up. When this happens,
however, employees can feel bad about themselves and less
inclined to confidently act on their own.

Encourage open dialogue and be available: Keep all communication channels honest and open. You need to be available for your employees so they can tell you their wants,
needs, fears, and challenges.

Remember, there are a lot of talents and skills to tap into
when it comes to your employees. Ultimately, giving employees praise, encouragement, and authority to make decisions is
how you can effectively embolden them to do their best, which
will, in turn, benefit your company in the short- and long-term.

USING TECHNOLOGY TO YOUR ADVANTAGE

Now more than ever, we are surrounded by technology. We
can't escape it—computers and other digital tools live both
at home and at work, and they're increasingly becoming part
of our everyday lives. If you aren't shifting away from archaic
technology and communications systems, not only are you
doing your teams a disservice, you're allowing competition to
have the upper hand.

Don't be like the managers who underestimate the power
of technology and the serious advantages it can provide. Get
familiar with what technology can do for your organization,
like:

- Dispersing information to all staff widely, and in
  near-real time
- Communicating with partners who specialize in
  manufacturing and development of products
- Building strong customer loyalty through online
  engagement

Some businesses buy a bunch of new programs, apps, or digital tools without considering the existing technology they have in the office. Other businesses get excited about implementing new technology and then fail to follow through. Even if you understand that technology is an investment necessary for business strategies, make sure to create a thorough plan of action for using it if you want to truly reap its benefits.

Step 1: Consider your company's values. Write these down.

Step 2: Visualize where your company will be a decade from now. What will change? Will your business be in the same industry? Will your staff grow in size?

Step 3: Decide on a significant one-year company goal and pursue it.

Step 4: Create a list of strategies (and assignments) for goal achievement.

Step 5: Hold a tactic brainstorming session in which you set milestones and deadlines.

Step 6: Figure out which technologies will best serve your tactics.

REVOLUTIONIZING YOUR BUSINESS

Some of today's most successful companies got that way by tearing down the roadblocks that still stand in the way of success for other companies. Consider the examples that follow as you think about how you can revolutionize your own business.

Costco

This company has taken a very public stance that they will keep their primary focus on their customers and their employees, reasoning that they will achieve business success if they have happy customers and an engaged workforce. The company pays warehouse workers very well, far above typical wages for retailers. Workers also receive very generous benefits by industry standards, including a healthcare plan that once attracted the ire of Wall Street analysts. Though some modest changes have been made since, Costco reaffirms its commitment to employees by maintaining a very generous program.

In addition to these economic advantages, Costco offers an environment that is rich in respect for individual workers. Warehouse managers are required to understand and develop their workforces. Leaders are routinely promoted from within rather than hired from outside the company. Terminating an employee requires significant review and approvals.

The result? Productivity and loyalty among Costco workers are at levels nearly unheard-of for the retail industry. Turnover is nearly nonexistent after employees have been with the company two years. Many people make Costco a career choice, contributing to the company's unique success.

Procter & Gamble (P&G)

In many ways, this company reinforces leadership's belief that people are the true creators of business success. The unique culture at P&G is, at its core, a strong statement of purpose, values, and principles. The top two principles are "We show respect for all individuals," and "The interests of the company and the individual are inseparable."[9] These principles are at the foundation of many programmatic efforts across P&G. Most important, they result in the broad-based acknowledgment that the company is truly an "employer of choice" for talented people.

Starbucks

Starbucks' perspective is that its employees are really business partners who are critical to customer satisfaction. Employees are called *partners,* and even the name of the HR department was changed to Partner Resources. This visible respect for the individual extends to the programs Starbucks offers: healthcare benefits for most partners and broad-based stock ownership through the Bean Stock program. In addition, the company pays close attention to the work environment because leadership understands that many of those working at Starbucks want a lively, fun place to spend time—as do many of Starbucks' customers.

Stonyfield Farm

The company's leaders strive to get employees to take care of the business as if it was their own. This is accomplished by giving employees the opportunity to enjoy the rewards of their hard work by sharing profits. Further, the company treats employees as important members of the team by opening their books to them—they know everything there is to know about Stonyfield Farm's financial position.

Toyota Motor Company

Even as it has grown, Toyota's people practices are grounded in a culture of respect for the individual. Many believe this stems from Toyota's roots in a small town, where leadership and workers lived side by side. Toyota's leaders could not ignore or overlook the capabilities and needs of the common worker.

The lean engineering approach adopted by Toyota and copied throughout the world reemphasizes this respect for the knowledge and capabilities of the front-line worker. Only by engaging those who do the work in finding ways to increase productivity can true change happen. Toyota and other lean-process organizations today are again calling upon the wisdom of their workers to advance.

15

Fail Faster (and Win Sooner!)

*Create "safe to fail" experiments and build
in quick feedback loops to understand if
we are achieving the desired outcomes.*

—BARRY O'REILLY, business advisor

You may run, and you may hide, but the reality is that at any moment, change will show up on your organization's front doorstep. Some try to stop it, some try to deny it, but no matter what, change will occur in your organization. It can happen in company structure, it can happen with individual workload. It can happen in small ways (a new protocol with client invoices) or it can happen in large, overwhelming ways (company relocation).

Most managers spend much of their working hours simply trying to fight change, to prepare and get a grip on it, and to prevent it from negatively affecting their organization. But these managers fail to remember something very important: businesses can benefit and flourish with change.

In truth, businesses—like people—*need* change. Change is what leads to better products, individual advancement in both career and personal life, and overall progress. Change isn't something to be afraid of—it's something to accept and even appreciate. In this chapter, we'll take a close look at change, and how to encourage employees to make good change happen in organizations by experimenting and taking risks.

WHAT ARE THE FOUR STAGES OF CHANGE?

Most of us probably think we know how change affects us. However, there are four definite stages that each of us goes through when we navigate any significant change in our lives. Problems occur when we get stuck at one of the stages instead of moving through all four.

Stage 1: Denial. Denial can be almost immediate once you get word that change is coming or that it has already arrived. Employees may doubt that the change will be implemented, and you may have trouble imagining a world without the old system in place. But just because you deny change or because you can't see the instant results of it does not mean change has not occurred.

Stage 2: Resistance. Resisting change is a completely typical way of responding to any sort of switch-up. We all resist change sometimes, but you must not get stuck because of this resistance. To move forward with old practices or old ways of doing things may be comfortable, but you should accept change so you may receive the benefits that it will bring.

Stage 3: Exploring change. At this point, you are starting to realize that new changes are valid, and that there is no value in denying or resisting what is happening. Now you may analyze the pros and cons of this change and decide how to navigate it. Progress is starting to occur.

Stage 4: Acceptance. Finally, you have accepted the change. It is now effectively worked into your routine and part of the status quo. You may even wonder why you ever rejected and denied it in the first place. Successfully completing this step prepares you for the next change, which will inevitably occur—perhaps sooner than you think.

WARNING SIGNS THAT YOU ARE RESISTING CHANGE

Sometimes we fight change without knowing it, and sometimes the people we manage do the same thing. If we resist change instead of embracing it, then our organizations will never get the full benefit from it.

Watch out for these seven warning signs of resistance. If any one of these warning signs is present, it's likely you or your employees are not accepting change as you should be to move your organization forward.

1. **Slowing things down:** Wanting to take time to assess and examine changes in order to decide on a response is normal, but if you take too much time, your organization's productivity can come crashing down.

2. **Avoiding new tasks:** New practices and changes at an organization may compel someone resistant to change to avoid assignments entirely because they are overwhelmed by the change or are simply uncomfortable with the unknown.

3. **Acting victimized:** When you play the role of the victim, it makes it easier for others to feel sorry for you, which can be both a comfortable and dangerous position to be in. However, your organization didn't hire a victim, so if change occurs, embrace it and leverage it to your benefit.

4. **Hoping someone else will take the initiative:** Years ago, regular employees weren't generally required to step up and take initiative during times of change. That was the job of management. When you or another person on your team is waiting for someone else to take initiative in the face of change, that's a sure sign of resistance to it.

5. **Using old rules and systems:** Change means playing a new game. And playing a new game means new rules. If you keep playing the old game using the old rules, you will be swiftly left behind.

6. **Trying to control what can't be controlled:** Don't waste energy trying to control the inevitable. Rather, focus your efforts on how to effectively respond to and leverage the changes that arrive.

7. **Letting change paralyze you:** This is the greatest sign that you are resisting change. If you think change is too overwhelming, you may give up altogether. You will fail to successfully respond to change and fail to perform your duties. Instead of becoming paralyzed by change, consider being a huge fan; embrace it and find ways to be flexible with it. Put your focus on the things you can accomplish, instead of the things you cannot. Continue to keep your employees involved and feeling valuable—acknowledge the workers who have learned to accept ongoing changes and have thrived as a result.

Solving a problem like being resistant to change requires you to recognize the signs in the first place. If you or your employees are showing any of these warning signs, you can do something. You can turn your attitudes about change around and make it work for you. After all, only when you are comfortable with embracing change will you have a better chance of gaining value from it.

ENCOURAGING EMPLOYEES TO STEP UP AND TAKE RISKS

At work, company-wide change doesn't affect only one person. It affects teams, departments, and often times, the organization as a whole. Because change is often never-ending—due to such things as shifting markets, technological advancements, and changing customer wants and needs—you must remember that employees will need your extra support in order to adjust to new environments. Here are some ways to do just that.

Urging Employees to Take Charge

Believe it or not, an employee who is given permission to be in charge of their own responsibilities and tasks is an employee who can effectively make it through big changes in the workplace. Encourage employees to step up and take charge—they will find ways to improve performance, and your organization will find success.

As a manager, it is your priority to make employees feel comfortable enough to take charge. Not only will office productivity benefit from this, but also employees will better weather any storm of change because of it. Here are some tips for encouraging employees to take charge:

- Ask employees to seek out potential improvements for work practices and policies, their department, or even the organization as a whole.

- If they need assistance, volunteer to help employees with implementing ideas.

- Have employees create a plan of action for follow-through.

- Suggest that employees focus on finding areas of improvement that would positively affect the organization the most.

Providing Empathy and Support

Change—especially a major change—is no joke. When a major change occurs, many people have trouble adequately adjusting or adapting to things that are drastically different than what they're used to. Provide empathy and support to your employees as they work through the change. They will appreciate that their boss cares about their well-being and will be more supportive of the change themselves. Here are some ways to provide empathy and support to your employees during times of change:

Train employees: When change hits, offer your workers in-house training on how to deal with change. One option is to also bring in an outside consultant specialized in this area.

Be communicative: As much as you can, give employees advanced notice regarding potential changes at work. Keep them updated so they won't be surprised by unexpected changes.

Avoid sugarcoating: Give your employees the truth. No one wants to be scared by upcoming changes or bad news, but no one wants false assurances, either.

Ask for feedback and involve employees: Communicate to employees that you would like their suggestions on how to deal with problems that may arise surrounding potential changes. Respond to feedback positively. You may even implement their ideas and delegate responsibilities for making decisions that have to do with changes.

Show that you care: Ultimately, you want to show your employees that you genuinely care about their state of being during times of instability in the business world. Be a good listener and encourage them to communicate their thoughts and concerns. Most of all, look ahead to a time when the organization will progress and grow once change is adapted to and even capitalized on.

Keeping Spirits High

Dramatic changes, such as staff downsizing, for example, can take a heavy toll on how secure or motivated employees feel. Keeping employee morale high is incredibly crucial during these times of heavy change. Employees will feel thrown off by job uncertainty during this time and they may be doing more work to cover for those who have been laid off. Here's how you can help keep everyone in good spirits no matter what change-ups are happening at the office:

Be frank and honest: When you hide the truth, employees will respect you less for not being straightforward and real. Tell your workers if an upcoming change will affect their jobs somehow. Don't postpone telling them the news until it's too late.

Put employees first: If you put employees at the top of the list of your priorities, they will realize this and show you better quality work, more perseverance, and increased loyalty. Give your employees 100 percent of yourself, and they will give you 110 percent in return.

Create and nurture a fun environment: An office in low spirits is not an office where work gets done or employees are happy. Inject fun into the normal office routine. Hold a beach day (complete with sand in the warehouse), a golf tournament with a course laid out through your offices, or schedule a day full of fun activities for all employees.

Be a leader: Now is your time to lead. Setting a good example means taking the initiative to perform well even when times get tough, and it means inspiring employees when you do so.

16

Leading a Diverse Workforce

Diversity is about all of us,
and about us having to figure out
how to walk through this world together.

—JACQUELINE WOODSON, author

*D*iversity, especially in the workplace, is no longer a much-discussed buzzword. With global communities—and businesses—becoming more and more diverse over time, diversity in staff, leaders, customers, and clients is a reality.

When we talk about *diversity* in a business setting, we're describing a workplace that reflects the wide variety of people in the world around us; this includes gender, ethnicity, sexual orientation, physical and mental ability, and so on. William Rothwell further explains that,

> Celebrating diversity means appreciating other people for who they are—regardless of factors that have nothing to do with performance, such as race, color, sex, religion, national origin, culture, physical or mental disability, age, sexual orientation, gender identity, veterans' status, or immigration status—and the

creative perspectives that different people may
bring to a group.[1]

When we recruit and retain a diverse workforce, we open
up our organizations to new ideas and new ways of thinking
that can increase their success. Not only that, but our organizations better reflect the world in which we do business—making our products and services better suited to our customers.

To find further and longer-lasting business success, it
is important to understand that although the current state
of the contemporary workforce boasts increased diversity,
there is still much to be improved. In fact, lack of equal treatment is still an area of concern in many businesses and other
organizations.

Sexual orientation: Because lesbian, gay, bisexual, and
transgender people have become more accepted at work, it
can be noted that workplace diversity has increased when it
comes to sexual orientation. However, Catalyst reports that
"one-fifth (20 percent) of LGBTQ Americans have experienced discrimination based on sexual orientation or gender identity when applying for jobs." Catalyst also reports
that "22 percent of LGBTQ Americans have not been paid
equally or promoted at the same rate as their peers."[2]

Race: According to a 2018 NBC News poll, 64 percent of
Americans said that racism remains a major problem in
our society today. At the same time, 45 percent of Americans believe that race relations in the United States are
getting worse, and 40 percent of African-Americans report
that they have been treated unfairly in a store or restaurant
because of their race over the last month. In addition, 25
percent of Hispanics reported being treated unfairly in a
store or restaurant over the last month, while just 7 percent
of whites did.[3]

Gender: According to a Catalyst report, although women
in 2017 held 51.6 percent of all positions in management,

professional, and related occupations, women are less represented the higher they go in the organization. In S&P 500 companies, for example, only 26.5 percent of executive/senior-level officials and managers, and 4.8 percent of CEOs, are women.[4]

Increasing diversity and workplace equality requires effort. You and your company must create and execute a plan that calls for a more diverse and inclusive hiring process. Encourage people of color to apply for positions and understand that an inclusive company will reap a happier, more creative, and innovative workplace. There are financial rewards as well. According to a Boston Consulting Group (BCG) study, companies that have more diverse management teams have 19 percent higher revenue. Why? Because they are more innovative than companies with management teams that are not diverse.[5]

THE DIVERSITY ADVANTAGE

We need to give each other the space to grow, to be ourselves, to exercise our diversity. We need to give each other space so that we may both give and receive such beautiful things as ideas, openness, dignity, joy, healing, and inclusion.

—MAX DE PREE, former CEO, Herman Miller

If your organization is not as diverse as it could or should be, then there are many reasons to make the case for inclusion and diversity. Initially, you may want to promote diversity to match industry standards for companies like yours, to accommodate social responsibilities, or to comply with legal requirements.

But you should also know that the most successful companies understand the real power and benefits of the inclusive and diverse workplace. They know that an inclusive business has a serious edge over competitors, and that leading

companies recognize the correlation between business performance and diversity.

A report issued by McKinsey & Company in 2018 points out
a number of reasons for making the business case for inclusion
and diversity:

Diversity matters. There is a statistically significant correlation between financial outperformance and more-
diverse leadership teams.

Gender diversity creates value. Businesses ranked in the
top-quartile for gender diversity on executive teams were
found to be 21 percent more likely to outperform on profitability and 27 percent more likely to be superior value
creators.

Ethnic and cultural diversity leads to greater profits.
Companies with executive teams in the top-quartile for
ethnic/cultural diversity were 33 percent more likely to lead
their industries in profitability.

Not participating means falling behind. There is an existing and persisting penalty for a company that performs
poorly when its diversity is measured. Companies in the
bottom quartile for ethnic/culture and gender diversity
are actually 29 percent less likely to garner profits that are
above average.[6]

Make no mistake about it, progress is being made. But this
progress is painfully slow. With some companies increasing
gender and cultural representation by single-digit percentage
points, other companies are still not effectively using inclusion
and diversity to reach growth goals and influence business
outcomes.

If you want your inclusive and diverse work environment to fully deliver an impact, communicate a compelling
vision that promotes inclusion and diversity and moves down
through middle management or that links growth strategies
to inclusion and diversity. Ultimately, you want to hardwire

a culture of inclusion and diversity into your organization's DNA. This will attract and retain top talent at your business and will improve customer service while boosting employee satisfaction.

TEARING DOWN BARRIERS TO DIVERSITY

Unfortunately, many company recruiters regularly face diversity obstacles in their organizations—creating barriers to attracting and retaining the very best people. Attaining diversity in the workplace is not as simple or natural as one would hope, but here are ways you can address and prevent many of the most common diversity issues in the workplace.

Resolve gender inequality: Men earn approximately 24.1 percent more than women in base pay, and women are 30 percent less likely to be promoted to a managerial role than men.[7] As an employer, prevent gender discrimination by ensuring equality when offering salary, when hiring, and when giving promotions and opportunities.

Accommodate physical and mental disabilities: Provide a fair physical work environment to create a diverse workforce. For example, proper accommodations like wheelchair ramps keep the workspace accessible for those who have certain physical limitations.

Bridge generational gaps: Be alert to the fact that organizations with more diversified age groups can stratify into cliques and social circles that isolate workers. Foster an open communication culture at your company to maintain teamwork across all ages.

Fix language/communication barriers: Common in diverse workforces, language and communication barriers can be fixed if language training is provided; this can reduce productivity loss and miscommunication.

Address cultural differences: Employees with different cultural, ethnic, or religious backgrounds can face prejudice in the workplace. This should never be tolerated, so make sure you implement diversity awareness programs, cultural sensitivities training, and internal company policies that prevent prejudice.

Accommodate all beliefs: A diverse workplace brings diverse cultural, political, and spiritual beliefs. Remind employees that they shouldn't impose their beliefs on others, and to keep these beliefs independent of their duties and tasks at work.

Accept and respect one another: Employees who acknowledge, understand, and accept their differences will find effective collaboration and mutual respect, rather than conflict in the workplace.

Remember, a company with a more diverse workforce has a clear benefit to the bottom line. As McKinsey reported, companies in the top quartile for ethnic and cultural diversity among their executive teams are 33 percent more likely to generate profitability in the top range of their industry.[8]

WOMEN IN BUSINESS

Even though progress has been made in closing gender gaps at work, myths about women in leadership and in business still exist, providing obstacles as a woman travels the road to success. Here are four common myths that you will need to watch out for:[9]

Men are more confident than women: Widely regarded as more self-assured and assertive than women, men actually experience self-doubt just as women do. And, just as men are perceived to be decisive, strong, skilled, and confident, just as many women are too. However, when women demonstrate confidence, this confidence can be mistaken for coldness or being conceited.

Women are less committed to work than men: This belief has stemmed from women being traditionally tasked with childcare at home. However, according to a Harvard survey, there is no gender difference when students give answers about their ambitions for corporate hierarchy and pay, or how many weekly hours they are willing to work.

Women don't support each other: "While I don't think catty behavior between women in the workplace is as prevalent as people often make it out to be," says Dr. Kellie McElhaney, professor at the Haas School of Business at the University of California, Berkeley, "there may sometimes be a grain of truth to it."[10] After all, competition in a male-dominated workforce does exist, and can be heavy. But women, often expected to be nice, are also perceived as "catty" whenever they are at odds or in disagreement with another woman. Celebrate women in public in order to fight this myth.

Women are overly emotional and dramatic: Because of this myth, women are thought to be unable to lead during times of crisis or pressure and are considered incapable of acting authoritatively. At the same, time, a man who raises his voice is regarded as powerful, not emotional. Beware of this bias.

These myths are not true by any means, but they still have real-world effects on a woman's professional life and career. As a manager, you should not only acknowledge that these hurdles exist for your women staff members and leaders, but you should ensure that these myths do not affect your decisions—whether in hiring, promoting, or otherwise.

ABOUT THOSE MILLENNIALS

Did you know that by 2020, half of the workforce will be comprised of Millennials? The Millennial generation—generally considered to be born between 1981 and 1996—has been "increasingly recognized as eager, ambitious, and genuinely talented," according to communication analyst Roshini

Rajkumar.[11] However, older generations may find it difficult to work with Millennials' work habits, expectations, and styles of communication.

Millennials are here to stay and will be occupying leadership positions soon (if they are not already). Here's how to successfully communicate with this generation and earn their respect—for your benefit and the benefit of your organization.

Be concise and meaningful: Millennials relate to a meaningful message that is brief. They're all too familiar with Twitter, where you have to keep your message to 280 characters or less, so they appreciate brevity. Skip unnecessary prose but be sure to still be detailed and thorough when the time calls for it.

Show workplace fairness: Millennials heavily value equality, and an even distribution of rights. Leaders and coworkers who want to communicate with Millennials should not exhibit any sort of prejudice or bias against any individuals or groups of people. They don't need jokes about their age, or condescending comments, so expect to take them seriously if you would like a sense of respect to be felt around the office.

Commit to the greater good: Is your company contributing to improving the world in some fashion? Does it participate in charitable giving? A social bottom line is one that will appeal to the Millennial generation.

Communicate a career path: Out of one surveyed group of twenty-five- to thirty-four-year-olds, 61 percent believe that, after two to three years of performing well, they should be promoted. Although they're a generation known for instant gratification through social media, it doesn't mean they don't plan for the long-term. Hold frequent performance assessments and inform junior employees what their path is within your company.

Encourage their purpose: Something particularly striking about members of this generation is their desire to lead mission-driven lives. Communicate to Millennials about company purpose, and their value and importance in accomplishing goals. They may feel like their passions are nurtured, and that they are performing work that *means* something.

Any leader of any age can learn how to effectively communicate with the Millennial generation. It just takes an understanding of Millennial values, workflow, and aspirations.

17

Surviving Politics and People

*You can make more friends in
two months by becoming interested in other
people than you can in two years by trying to
get other people interested in you.*

—DALE CARNEGIE, author

Office politics—the behaviors people use to gain and keep power on the job—is something that occurs to varying degrees in every organization. Some organizations are relatively free of office politics, while others are immersed in it. Office politics finds a particularly fertile ground to grow in environments where people are, for whatever reason, insecure, and openness and personal growth are not priorities.

In one sense, office politics can be a good thing. It can help you build stronger relationships with others throughout the organization, and it can help you build a network that enables you to get more things done through others. As a manager, for example, you might reach out to other managers in other departments to build better working relationships. This could involve scheduling meetings with them in your office to discuss issues or opportunities of mutual interest or taking them out for informal get-acquainted lunches or dinners.

This is good office politics because it is used to achieve positive outcomes for all. Everyone is working together to advance the organization and build up the people who work for and with them.

However, in another sense, office politics can be a bad thing. And that's generally what we're talking about when we describe a department or business that has been disrupted by office politics. This is a place where trust is broken between everyone—not just between managers and employees, but between people at every level. Bosses play favorites, employees compete against one another instead of cooperating, gossip is pervasive, envy and dishonesty are unchecked, brownnosing is rampant, and drama kings and queens rule the roost.

When office politics gets to this abysmally low point, businesses and the people in them suffer tremendously. Software and technology authority Better Buys conducted a research study across a wide swath of industries into the kinds of bad behavior most commonly engaged in by employees. In many cases, this bad behavior is a direct result of the bad kind of office politics. Here are the top ten bad behaviors according to the Better Buys survey:

1. Consistently late (54.8 percent)
2. Gossiping behind someone's back (53.7 percent)
3. Taking a sick day when not sick (53.2 percent)
4. Yelling at someone (51 percent)
5. Socializing excessively (49.2 percent)
6. Taking an unauthorized long lunch break (42.8 percent)
7. Leaving early without permission (41.4 percent)
8. Lying to the boss (41.1 percent)
9. Practicing bad hygiene (37.4 percent)
10. Working on personal projects at work (35.3 percent)[1]

At its best, office politics helps you develop the relationships with your coworkers—both up and down the chain of command—that allow you to get tasks done, to be informed about the latest goings-on in the business, and to form a personal network of business associates for support throughout your career. At its worst, office politics can degenerate into a competition, where employees concentrate their efforts on trying to increase their personal power at the expense of other employees—and their organizations.

But it's not just employees who exhibit the bad behaviors that result when office politics gets out of control. According to the Better Buys survey, bosses act badly too. Here are the top-ten boss bad behaviors reported by survey respondents:

1. Yelled at someone (37 percent)
2. Used foul language (profanity) (20.8 percent)
3. Gossiped behind someone's back (18.9 percent)
4. Socialized excessively (17.4 percent)
5. Taken credit for someone else's work (15.2 percent)
6. Left early without permission (13.7 percent)
7. Taken a sick day when they weren't sick (13.5 percent)
8. Taken a long lunch without permission (13.2 percent)
9. Been consistently late (11.7 percent)
10. Told inappropriate jokes (racist, off-color, etc.) (11.7 percent)[2]

How office politics is played where you work will have a direct impact on your long-term happiness and success and on the happiness and success of those who work for and with you. Because office politics is so common, and so important, the sooner you get familiar with the politics of your office or organization the better.

NINE SIGNS THAT OFFICE POLITICS IS OUT OF CONTROL

Politics is a natural part of any office. It's not normally something you'll need to worry much about as a manager unless it gets out of control and employees, customers, and the bottom line start to get hurt by it. That's when you'll need to step in and take action to stop the negative effects of office politics.

Those who practice destructive office politics like to do their work in the shadows, hiding behind others. Shine a very bright light on anyone who practices destructive office politics and call them out whenever you encounter this. Don't allow rumors and innuendo to grow and fester—cut them off at the pass every time.

The American Management Association recently published a list of nine signs of an organization that has too much office politics going on:

Problem #1: Gridlock. Your company is at a standstill because no one can agree on what to do.

Problem #2: Bureaucracy. People are so bogged down in paperwork, red tape, and stifling rules that their progress is impeded.

Problem #3: Grandstanding (aka brownnosing). People pay lip service to leaders' ideas to flatter and curry favor with them, but have no real commitment to implementing change.

Problem #4: The two-faced two-step. People say what they think the people they're talking to at the moment want to hear.

Problem #5: Passing the buck. No one takes responsibility for anything; people are quick to assign blame to someone else.

Problem #6: Laziness, clockwatching, and poor work ethic. People have a sense of entitlement; they're just "putting in face time" until they can go home.

Problem #7: Indirect communication. Instead of talking to coworkers directly when they have a problem, employees complain to supervisors and talk about people behind their backs.

Problem #8: Pork-barreling. Influential employees push through expensive projects that serve only one small part of the company.

Problem #9: Corruption. People are actually embezzling from the company, fudging reports, or engaging in other unethical or illegal behavior.[3]

WHO ARE THE KEY PLAYERS?

Now that you have learned the practices and behavioral rules of your office, you can begin navigating your political office environment. However, you must also learn the key individuals in your office who positively affect productivity and workplace morale. These are the people who get things done. They might not have high-level positions, but they do have high-level influence. They are very accomplished at playing office politics.

These key players usually fall into certain categories of people. Can you identify who is who in your office? Which kind of key player are you?

The experts: Individuals who are technically competent and can take the lead in difficult situations.

Firefighters: These people love stepping in to save projects at the last minute.

The vetoer: Keep this person out of your decision-making process, as they often kill ideas at the drop of a hat.

Whiners: These employees are pessimists and are almost never happy with the work done for them.

Gossipers: This group is always in the know and is aware of office news well before everyone else.

Corporate citizens: These employees are dependable, incredible resources, and seek long-term advancement in the company.

Movers and shakers: An individual in this category is highly skilled and typically performs duties well beyond the limits of their position.

HOW DOES YOUR ORGANIZATION REALLY OPERATE?

Every organization is different—no two operate in exactly the same way. If you're new to management, or new to your organization, it's in your interest to find out exactly how your organization actually operates. That is, what is the culture, what are the customs, what are the ground rules that you'll need to navigate to be successful?

Although you may have worked for a business for quite some time, when you become a new manager, you're going to have an entirely new perspective on how the organization works. It's sort of like journeying to a foreign country. If you want to be comfortable during the course of your visit, no matter how short or long it may be, you'll need to gain some amount of knowledge about the culture, customs, and ground rules that you'll need to follow.

Here are some tried-and-true ways to better understand how your organization operates, and how you'll fit in it as a manager:

Ask your coworkers insightful questions. Not only does this reveal you as a mature and polite employee with foresight, but answers will give you useful knowledge. One example of such a question would be, "What's the best way to get this budget approved?"

Learn the practices of the organization's most effective workers. Do you know how the most productive employees complete their tasks? Do they delegate certain task items? How do they manage time?

Pay attention to how and why employees are rewarded and disciplined. When you observe the rewards and discipline system of your company, you can learn what behavior is expected of employees and what behavior is considered unacceptable.

Observe how formal staff members act. Can you state your thoughts without fear of stepping on anyone's toes?

Do you need to adjust the language you use? How formal an organization is will tell you how you should behave in front of others.

THE COMMUNICATION CONUNDRUM

As you no doubt realize by now, what is said in an organization can have a deeper, underlying meaning. When you read between the lines, acquire background context and information, and pay attention to the behavior of others, that's when you can decipher the real message behind what is communicated.

Some people place heavy value and meaning on the tools they use to communicate. Be cautious. These tools can actually suggest a person's deep insecurities about power and success. For example, a Rolex watch may tell your employee the time, but it also tells you that the person wearing it wants attention. Or, consider a fancy and expensive smart phone—the one that rings during meetings, that allows the owner to frequently excuse themselves from the room in order to deal with a so-called important client. This tool can be used most anytime by a person who wants to appear busy and popular with customers.

When it comes to written business matters, you will have to do a lot of reading between the lines. Even if you think you are fully aware of what is going on, the reality may be that there is some information you do not know about just yet.

For example, suppose an announcement about a long-standing employee departing from the company is sent out in a mass email to all staff. Although the announcement reads as logical and straightforward, you may be able to read between the lines using background information, to understand what the announcement is really saying. You could conclude that this former employee, who the boss had been trying to fire for a while, had finally done something that led to termination. Naturally, it is imperative that you do not make it a habit of jumping to conclusions, because you might not always be correct.

There are ways, however, to confirm your conclusions—you just need to know how to successfully probe for information. Become a trusted listener and others will openly talk about themselves, especially after you show a genuine regard for their interests. After creating these relationships, you can start to inquire about the information (rumors, intel on upcoming events or decisions, etc.) you seek. Make sure you confirm that the information is true with multiple sources, that you act casual when you ask questions, and that you ask questions in different ways.

If you want to further understand the real meaning behind what a person says, believe their actions more than their words. Someone can say one thing, sure, but do their values and priorities match what they said? If your manager keeps saying that they are working on increasing your paid time off, do you notice any concrete moves (calls to higher-ups, submitted paperwork) made that back up her statements? Remember: a communicator's spoken messages are important, but so are their actions.

The rules and guidelines an organization follows are often written down and help guide employee performance and workplace operations. At the same time, there is always an existing set of unwritten rules that are still critically important in any business or organization. Unwritten rules speak to the way employees behave, and what is expected of them. They can make or break a person's career, depending on how these rules are followed. And, of course, they aren't documented anywhere—thus, you will have to do some digging for them on your own by asking insightful questions, observing others, and examining company resources. Here are other methods for uncovering your organization's unwritten rules.

Making Friends

Don't walk alone. If more and more people in your organization trust you, you will have a better work experience. Your immediate work group is rich with potential friendships, friendships that can grow both inside and outside the office. You can then expand your friendship circle to other departments of your organization.

Broaden your network by simply walking around the office and chatting up anyone you come across, joining committees (which typically have new people you can meet and converse with in an informal setting), or attending company functions (like team sports or day trips). Ultimately, it's nice to have friends at work. Plus, more friendships in the workplace will help get you any information you need, as well as build your contact list. Remember: you might actually end up working *for* some of these friends in some capacity in the near future!

Offering a Helping Hand

As some very wise person once said, you get what you give. Office politics dictates that when you give other people what they want, it will be easier for you to get what you're after. Attain the approval and assistance of your peers by demonstrating how valuable of an asset you are. Do they know what you bring to the table? Are your coworkers aware of all that they can gain when they help you?

There are a number of benefits you can provide to others in exchange for their help. These include information that not everyone knows, a returned favor, extra money to allocate to their budget, or a personal recommendation to company higher-ups. As you help others, make sure you are still following company policy. Avoid doing something unethical or breaking the law!

Drawing the Line

If you think a social event gives you a real opportunity where everyone in the organization is on the same level, where professional hierarchies are removed—consider getting rid of this belief entirely. Social functions are actually the kind of occasion where you must draw a line that you will not cross. Exercise caution at company events because you can damage your reputation and your career if you are not careful. All it takes is drinking a little too much, sexually harassing a coworker at the company holiday party, or being too social and saying the wrong thing in front of the wrong person.

Instead, practice poise. Keep conversations light and be properly involved in discussions. If alcohol is offered, either drink lightly or not at all. Avoid talking about work, and only exit a social function after the boss leaves. You may be at a company party, but don't actually engage in serious partying.

Managing Up

Did you know that employees are not the only ones who should be managed? Managers should also be managed. This means that managers should be encouraged to make moves that benefit not only staff members but you as well. Here are some highly effective manager management strategies:

Have your manager's back during staff meetings: "Richard is absolutely correct in his assessment. We really should think about the effect this change will have on our monthly services."

Don't be shy about mentioning your successes: "This new client I landed is going to bring us our most profitable deal of the quarter."

Publicly commend your manager: "I have never had a manager as knowledgeable and skilled as Theresa—she's the best."

Be sure to form good relationships with any top-level staff members above your manager in company hierarchy. A strong relationship with your manager's manager can only bode well for your career in the long term.

DEALING WITH TOXIC EMPLOYEES

We've all worked with people who are so negative—both in their attitudes and their actions—that there's nothing else to call them but *toxic*. Toxic employees can suck the energy right out of an organization and out of the people who work in it. A few years ago, I wrote an article for Inc.com that describes the seven toxic employees you need to get out of your life as soon as you can.[4]

Although you may not actually want to get these employees out of your life—chances are they are providing value to your business—you can and should do everything you can to reduce the toxicity they bring to the workplace. Have you seen these seven toxic people in your office lately?

1. **The one who pushes their problems onto everyone else.**

   Have you ever worked with someone who tries to get you to do *their* job in addition to your own? This kind of employee is an expert at finding ways—often *sneaky* ways—to get their coworkers to do their jobs for them. These people never seem to get anything done, but they constantly complain that they are overworked and underpaid. The best cure for this toxic employee is to be sure you set definite goals with quantitative measures, and then regularly determine whether or not the employee is meeting them. If the employee isn't, then they may be due for an attitude correction.

2. **The one who says, "Oh well, that's their problem."**

   There should never be a job or situation at work that is someone else's problem. Even if something crosses someone's desk that they normally don't handle, they should always take the responsibility to find the right person to handle it as efficiently and effectively as possible.

3. **The one who constantly yells or loses their temper with clients and coworkers.**

   This kind of negative behavior is simply not acceptable. Show employees who can't control their temper the door.

4. **The one who always takes meetings off track.**

   You know the one—the employee who seems to love nothing more than talking about anything else in a meeting besides whatever is on your agenda. Don't allow negative employees to ruin your meetings.

5. **The one who everyone else complains about.**

   When several employees are complaining about a particular coworker, there's a good chance you've got a negative employee on your hands. Instead of ignoring the complaints, check them out—and then take action if necessary.

6. **The one who says, "That's not my job." or "This is stupid."**

   An employee who consistently demonstrates this kind of attitude is not an employee who deserves a job—certainly not in your business.

7. **The one who is clearly unhappy.**

   Unhappy employees aren't good for you, your business, your customers, or anyone else. They make everyone around them unhappy, too, and that's bad for your business. Help them find happiness by getting them out of your business and on to new opportunities as quickly as possible.

No one likes to work around overly negative or toxic people. However, they may have no choice if they want to keep their job. Instead of fighting, they just do their best to ignore the negative behavior of the toxic people in the office—hoping that someone will address it, or it will miraculously just go away. Unfortunately, toxic people and the negative effect they have on organizations and the people around them don't often just go away.

No matter how much people stress positive energy, there will always be those around us that seem to weigh us down with their negativity. In fact, some people seem to revel in their pessimism, and they like nothing better than to spread it around. As a manager, you need to be alert to toxic employees in your organization, and you must take action to neutralize their effect on the people around them.

Your employees are looking to *you* to address this problem, and if you choose to ignore it, then a number of other negative consequences will cascade from your decision. Here are five things you can do to help turn people with negative energy into people with positive energy:

Empathize with their situation. We all feel down from time to time—we all know what it's like to be caught up in a negative situation from which we can see no clear path of escape. No one thinks, "I want to do a bad job at work today" when they get out of bed in the morning. Empathize with the negative person in front of you and try to get to the root of what's making them feel that way. Are they having relationship problems with a spouse or loved one at home? Are they angry because a coworker was promoted over them? Are they frustrated because a customer pulled an order at the last minute? If you dig deep enough, being empathetic as you dig, you'll likely find out where the negativity comes from. Once you figure that out, you'll be able to help do something about it.

Talk, but don't try to solve the problem yourself. Negative people often make lots of noise and ruckus in their organizations because this is the way they can release the pressure they are feeling. If other people get caught up in the pressure release, they think, that's just too bad for them. As a manager, you should listen to your negative employee and probe to get to the heart of what's making them so negative. However, draw the line at actually trying to solve the problem yourself. Ultimately, if your employee is going to turn his or her negative attitude into a positive one, then they're the ones who will have to solve the problems that are causing it. Be a good sounding board for your employees and encourage them to change their behavior.

Tap into their passions. There are things in our work lives that pique our passions. You might, for example, want to create and sell products that make people's lives better. I might, on the other hand, want to create the most amazing PowerPoint presentations you've ever seen. It's possible that at least part of the reason your negative employee is so negative is because they do not have the opportunity to do things on the job that tap into and release their passions. As a manager, you can do something about that. First figure out what unleashes your employee's passions, then give them assignments or responsibilities that provide them with the opportunity to exercise them. You will both be happier.

Listen between the lines. Sure, negative people tend to spew a lot of negative words wherever they go—inflaming the people around them. However, all that negativity might in reality be their way of coping with some really difficult challenges they are facing in their lives. The negativity might also be a cry for help from someone who feels overwhelmed by their work or career. As you listen to your negative employee talk, try to pinpoint what might be motivating those particular words and emotions, and what you can do to help the employee channel them into more positive feelings. Build your employee up and express how much you appreciate the good work they do. Help them build the self-confidence that they need to thrive in their job.

Get a smile. Even negative people get tired of being negative all the time. They would rather be positive and have fun with their coworkers and customers. Find out what makes your employee feel good. Are they proud of the accomplishments of their children? Do they like to spend time with their coworkers after work? Do they have a favorite place they like to visit? Figure out what puts a smile on your negative employee's face and see if you can get it to appear.

THE ETHICS QUESTION

Are you following a code of ethics at work? Are your daily business practices and deals infused with behavior that's fair and ethical, or do they somehow miss the mark? What about the people in your department, your organization—is their behavior consistent with the organization's published or implicit core values? With your own?

You will encounter moral challenges in every area of your business life as you move forward with your career. Someone will ask you to cut a corner here, bend a rule there, ignore a quality issue, "forget" to refund a customer's money, or withdraw a fully qualified job candidate from consideration because of their race or gender. You might even be asked—or ordered—to break the law.

Are you prepared to face these ethical dilemmas when they arise? What will you do?

What would you do if you sold a customer a product that you later found out was defective? Would you immediately contact the customer to warn them of the fault and encourage a refund or exchange, or would you ignore the problem and hope for the best? And, what if your boss told you to simply forget and ignore this knowledge about the product's faults? Then what would you do?

As a manager, your job will require you to regularly make ethical choices. The kind of decision you make in these situations will depend in great part on your own moral compass. What are your values, and are you willing to compromise them to please your boss or to avoid being fired? What are the red lines that you will never cross, no matter how much pressure is applied to you, and where do things get a bit fuzzy?

Someone with high ethical standards will usually embody these specific values at work, and in their personal lives:

- Fairness
- Honesty
- Loyalty
- Accountability
- Integrity
- Dedication
- Responsibility

Most companies today publish their core values, just as they publish their vision and mission statements. These core values serve as guardrails for employee ethical behavior. Here, for example, are the published core values of a few of today's most successful businesses:

COCA-COLA

- Leadership (The courage to shape a better future)
- Passion (Committed in heart and mind)
- Integrity (Be real.)
- Accountability (If it is to be, it's up to me.)
- Collaboration (Leverage collective genius.)
- Innovation (Seek, imagine, create, delight.)
- Quality (What we do, we do well.)
- Diversity (As inclusive as our brands)[5]

THE HOME DEPOT

- Excellent customer service
- Taking care of our people
- Building strong relationships

- Respect for all people
- Entrepreneurial spirit
- Doing the right thing
- Giving back
- Creating shareholder value[6]

APPLE

- Environment (To ask less of the planet, we ask more of ourselves.)
- Supplier responsibility (A supply chain that empowers people and protects the planet)
- Accessibility (Technology is most powerful when it empowers everyone.)
- Privacy (Apple products are designed to protect your privacy.)
- Inclusion and diversity (Open)[7]

When your company publishes its own set of core values like these successful companies do, then it's quite easy to know what decision to make when you're faced with an ethical dilemma. But what should you do if your company doesn't have its own set of core values, or if your boss or someone else is trying to get you to bend (or break) the rules? In that case, you'll need to turn to your own personal set of core values and use them as a guide for your behavior.

If you're looking to improve the choices you make, consider these simple steps.

Step 1: Evaluate the situation at hand, using different filters (What are the circumstances considering the culture? Law? Politics? Emotions?).

Step 2: Treat all parties and issues involved fairly. Make sure boundaries are established.

Step 3: Hesitate before you make serious decisions.

Step 4: Inform all involved in the situation of the decision that you make.

Step 5: Create a stable and consistent environment for yourself and employees.

Step 6: Seek any counsel you may need from someone who is honest and respectable.

And if you're looking to improve the ethical choices your employees make, then the best thing to do is to build a culture of courage in your organization. Don't punish your people for making ethical choices or for making choices that are consistent with the stated core values of your company.

Neutralize or remove the sources of pressure and fear that make good people decide to do bad things. In some cases, this may be disciplining or firing people who consistently bring bad ethical behavior with them to work.

Finally, praise, recognize, and reward employees who choose to do the right thing. Remember: you really do get what you reward.

GLOSSARY:
Essential Terms Every Manager Should Know

Accounts payable. Money owed to the people and organizations that have provided goods or services to your organization.

Accounts receivable. Money owed to your organization by clients and customers that have bought your goods or services.

Acid test. A measure of the ability of a business to pay its current liabilities out of its current assets minus inventory—also known as *quick ratio.*

Acquisition. When one business buys another business.

Actionable. Something that you can take action on.

Agile. An iterative project management methodology that values human communication and feedback, adapting to changes, and producing working results.

Assets. Cash and things of value that can be converted to cash, such as buildings, equipment, and inventory.

B2B (Business to business). Commerce and transactions directly between businesses.

B2C (Business to consumer). Commerce and transactions between businesses and consumers.

Balance sheet. A snapshot of your organization's financial health at a specific point in time, showing assets, liabilities, and owner's equity.

Benchmark. A standard used as a point of reference for measuring or judging quality or performance.

Bottom line. A business's net income—its income minus all expenses.

Budget. An estimate of income and expenditures for a specific period of time, such as a month, quarter, or year.

Buyout. When someone's ownership equity or majority share of stock is purchased.

Career-limiting move. Doing something bad that could limit any future promotions.

Cash flow. A comparison of an organization's cash inflows versus its cash outflows.

Compensation. The total of what an employee is paid for his or her work, including salary and benefits such as healthcare and sick leave.

Competitive advantage. When a business is in a position to outperform its competitors.

Core competencies. The skills and resources that distinguish a business in the marketplace.

Cost-benefit analysis. Weighing the costs of taking a specific course of action against the benefits.

Deep dive. Examining a business proposal or results in great detail.

Downsize. To reduce the size of an organization by decreasing the number of employees who work for it—also known as *right size*.

Due diligence. Conducting a thorough examination of the terms of a business transaction or agreement before executing it.

Fiscal year. A one-year period used for tax or accounting purposes—may or may not correspond to a standard calendar year.

Fixed assets. Assets that take more than one year to convert into cash, such as buildings and real estate.

Gain traction. Become more popular.

Gap analysis. A comparison of actual performance versus expected performance. Also known as *variance analysis.*

Goal setting. The process of deciding what you want to achieve and then creating a plan to achieve it.

Income statement. *See* profit and loss statement.

Lean. The process of organizing business activities in a way that delivers increased value to customers while reducing waste.

Liabilities. Money owed to people or organizations outside your own organization.

Low-hanging fruit. Easiest targets or goals to accomplish with minimal effort.

Net income. *See* bottom line.

Organizational development (OD). A planned and systematic approach to improving organizational effectiveness, often through employee training programs, coaching, change management, and more.

Outplacement. Helping employees find new jobs after a downsizing or layoff.

Peter Principle. When someone is promoted to a position that is higher than their capability or expertise.

Profit. A business's financial gain, calculated by subtracting total expenses from total revenues.

Profit and loss statement (P&L). A financial statement that adds a business's revenues and subtracts its expenses to determine its net income or net loss for a particular period of time—also known as an income statement.

Quick ratio. *See* acid test.

Revenue. The money a business brings in from selling its goods or services.

Right size. *See* downsize.

ROI (Return on investment). The number of dollars of net income earned for each dollar of invested capital.

Six Sigma. A system for eliminating product defects and improving business processes using statistical tools and analysis.

SME (Subject matter expert). Someone who possesses an expert understanding or skills in a particular subject or process.

Think outside the box. Thinking outside your standard paradigm in uncommon ways in hopes of arriving at a creative idea or solution.

TQM (Total quality management). A system for continuous improvement of an organization's products and services.

Turnover. When employees leave an organization for any reason, including resigning, downsizing, and termination.

Variance analysis. *See* gap analysis.

Whitewater change. A fast-changing and unpredictable business environment.

Notes

INTRODUCTION

1. Rebecca L. Ray, "For CEOs, It's Still About Developing Leaders," *Global Leadership Forecast 2018* (Bridgeville, PA:DDI, 2018), 4.
2. Jack Zenger, "We Wait Too Long to Train Our Leaders," *Harvard Business Review,* December 17, 2012, hbr.org.
3. Peter Economy, "LinkedIn Just Revealed the 4 Traits of Really Bad Bosses (And Here's How to Fix Them)," Inc., October 16, 2018, www.inc.com.
4. Paul Petrone, "The Most Frustrating Thing a Boss Can Do Is . . . ," LinkedIn Learning, October 22, 2018, learning.linkedin.com.

CHAPTER 2

1. Peter Economy, "Forget SMART Goals—Try CLEAR Goals Instead," Inc. January 3, 2015, www.inc.com.

CHAPTER 4

1. Peter M. Senge, "The Leader's New Work: Building Learning Organizations," *MIT Sloan Management Review,* October 5, 1990, sloanreview.mit.edu.
2. Senge, "Leader's New Work."
3. Evgeny Morozov, "Form and Fortune," New Republic, February 22, 2012, newrepublic.com.

CHAPTER 5

1. Microsoft, "Survey Finds Workers Average Only Three Productive Days Per Week," Microsoft, March 15, 2005, news.microsoft.com.
2. Robert Half International, "Meeting of the Minds: Workers and Executives Dread Wasted Time, Disengagement," Robert Half International Inc., July 31, 2018, rh-us.mediaroom.com.

CHAPTER 6

1. James MacGregor Burns, *Leadership* (New York: Harper & Row, 1978), 2.
2. Gil Amelio, "Developing Excellent Communication . . . ," AZQuotes. com, Wind and Fly LTD, 2019. www.azquotes.com, accessed August 30, 2019.
3. Bob Nelson, "Managing and Motivating Virtual Workers," Incentive: What Motivates, January 22, 2019, www.incentivemag.com.
4. Starbucks, "Starbucks to Eliminate Plastic Straws Globally by 2020," Starbucks Stories and News, July 9, 2018, stories.starbucks.com.
5. Harvey Seifter and Peter Economy, Leadership Ensemble: Lessons in Collaborative Management from the World's Only Conductorless Orchestra (New York: Times Books, 2001), 15–16.

CHAPTER 7

1. Sangeeta Bharadwaj Badal and Bryant Ott, "Delegating: A Huge Management Challenge for Entrepreneurs," Gallup Business Journal, April 14, 2015, news.gallup.com.

CHAPTER 8

1. Peter Drucker, The Five Most Important Questions You Will Ever Ask About Your Organization (San Francisco: Jossey-Bass, 2008) xii.
2. Interact/Harris Poll, "Interact Report: The Top Complaints from Employees about Their Employers," Interact Authentic Communication, July 2015, interactauthentically.com.
3. Rick Garlick, "Managing Your Boss: The Impact of Manager Personality and Style on Employee Performance," Hospitalitynet, September 3, 2007, www.hospitalitynet.org.

CHAPTER 10

1. Sarah Payne, "6 New Stats for Employee Recognition Skeptics," Workhuman [Blog], November 14, 2017, resources.globoforce.com.
2. Chad Halvorson, "What Today's Employees Want from Their Managers," When I Work [blog], February 19, 2013, wheniwork.com.
3. Halvorson, "What Employees Want."

CHAPTER 14

1. Gallup, "From the Chairman and CEO," *State of the American Workplace* (Gallup, Inc., 2017), 2, www.gallup.com. Accessed August 16, 2019.

2. Susan Sorenson and Keri Garman, "How to Tackle U.S. Employees' Stagnating Engagement," Gallup Business Journal, June 11, 2013, news .gallup.com.

3. Gallup, "Chairman and CEO," 3.

4. Shelley Plieter, "Engaging Employees: Queen's Partnership with Aon Hewitt Celebrates 10 Years of Helping Small- and Medium-Sized Companies Succeed," Smith Magazine, Winter 2014, smith.queensu.ca.

5. Corporate Leadership Council, "Driving Performance and Retention Through Employee Engagement," CLC Executive Summary, 2004, www.stcloudstate.edu.

6. Corporate Leadership Council, "Driving Performance and Retention."

7. Indeed Editorial Team, "Report: Remote Work Can Bring Benefits, But Attitudes Are Divided," Indeed Blog, November 14, 2018, blog .indeed.com.

8. Ryan Pendall, "Tomorrow Half Your Company Is Quitting (So Win Them Back)," Gallup Workplace, December 4, 2017, www.gallup.com.

9. P&G, "Purpose, Value, and Principles: Our Foundation," Procter and Gamble, www.pg.com. Accessed September 4, 2019.

CHAPTER 16

1. William Rothwell, The Manager's Guide to Maximizing Employee Potential: Quick and Easy Strategies to Develop Talent Every Day (New York: AMACOM 2009), 172.

2. Catalyst, "Quick Take: Lesbian, Gay, Bisexual, and Transgender Workplace Issues, June 17, 2019, www.catalyst.org.

3. Andrew Arenge, Stephanie Perry, and Dartunorro Clark, "Poll: 64 Percent of Americans Say Racism Remains a Major Problem," NBC News, May 29, 2018, www.nbcnews.com.

4. Catalyst, "Quick Take: Women in the Workforce—United States," June 5, 2019, www.catalyst.org.

5. Anna Powers, "A Study Finds That Diverse Companies Produce 19 Percent More Revenue," Forbes, June 27, 2018, www.forbes.com.

6. Vivian Hunt, Sara Prince, Sundiatu Dixon-Fyle, and Lareina Yee, "Delivering through Diversity," McKinsey & Company (January 2018) 1.

7. Angela Hood, "7 Biggest Diversity Issues in The Workplace," This Way Global, blog, www.thiswayglobal.com. Accessed August 16, 2019.

8. Hunt et al. "Delivering through Diversity."

9. Kellie McElhaney, "Four Myths That (Still) Get in the Way of Women and Leadership," Haas School of Business, Berkeley MBA Blog, September 4, 2018, blogs.haas.berkeley.edu.

10. McElhaney, "Four Myths."
11. Michael Dimock, "Defining Generations: Where Millennials End and Generation Z Begins," Pew Research Center: Fact Tank, January 17, 2019, www.pewresearch.org; Roshini Rajkumar, "Communicating with Millennials in the Workforce," Roshini Performance Group: Roshini's Blog, October 7, 2015, roshinigroup.com.

CHAPTER 17

1. Better Buys, "Employees Behaving Badly: What's Really Happening at the Office," www.betterbuys.com. Accessed August 16, 2019.
2. Better Buys, "Employees Behaving Badly."
3. Joanne G. Sujansky, "Corporate Politics 101: The Nine Signs of an Overly Political Organization," American Management Association (AMA), January 24, 2019, www.amanet.org.
4. Peter Economy, "These Are the 7 Toxic Employees You Should Fire Right Now (Before It's Too Late)," Inc.: Leadership Guy Blog, September 5, 2017, www.inc.com.
5. The Coca-Cola Company, "Why Work at the Coca-Cola Company?" www.coca-colacompany.com. Accessed August 16, 2019.
6. The Home Depot, "Your Culture, Your Community: Living Our Values Every Day," careers.homedepot.com. Accessed August 16, 2019.
7. "Apple Site Map: Apple Values," Apple, www.apple.com. Accessed August 16, 2019.

About the Author

Peter Economy is a best-selling business author, ghost-writer, developmental editor, and publishing consultant with more than one hundred books to his credit (and more than two million copies sold). He writes columns on leadership and management for Inc.com (The Leadership Guy) and served for eighteen years as Associate Editor for *Leader to Leader* magazine, published by the Frances Hesselbein Leadership Forum. Peter taught "MGT 453: Creativity and Innovation" as a lecturer at San Diego State University, is on the National Advisory Council of The Art of Science Learning, and is a founding board member of SPORTS for Exceptional Athletes.

A graduate of Stanford University (with majors in Economics and Human Biology), Peter has worked closely with some of the nation's top business, leadership, and technology thinkers, including Jim Collins, Frances Hesselbein, Barry O'Reilly, Peter Senge, Kellie McElhaney, Jeff Patton, Marshall Goldsmith, Marty Cagan, Lolly Daskal, Guy Kawasaki, Emma Seppala, William Taylor, Jim Kilts, Jean Lipman-Blumen, Stephen Orban, Ken Blanchard, and many others.

Visit Peter at . . .

www.petereconomy.com
www.inc.com/author/peter-economy
@bizzwriter (Twitter)